# JOAN CRAWFORD
# My Way of Life

—◆—

SIMON AND SCHUSTER · NEW YORK

THIRD PRINTING

*"Desiderata," copyright 1927 by Max Ehrmann, copyright renewed 1954 by Bertha K. Ehrmann. Reprinted by permission Crescendo Publishing Company, Boston, Massachusetts.*

SBN 671–20970–1
LIBRARY OF CONGRESS CATALOG CARD NUMBER: 70-154098
DESIGNED BY EVE METZ
MANUFACTURED IN THE UNITED STATES OF AMERICA
PRINTED BY THE MURRAY PRINTING CO., FORGE VILLAGE, MASS.
BOUND BY AMERICAN BOOK-STRATFORD PRESS, NEW YORK, N.Y.

I WOULD LIKE to thank Audrey Davenport Inman who for several months kept hitting me over my head to make me sit down at my tape recorder and finish dictating this book. It's not easy to produce a book when you're doing two other full-time jobs, but Audrey made me do it. My head is still sore. I appreciate her expertise in organizing it and her persistence in making me edit it.

A GREAT MANY of the photographs in this book were taken by Thecla and Joseph Griffith, and some by Wendy Hilty, and I am very grateful to them for their permission to reproduce them here.

# CONTENTS

## Part One · MY WAY OF LIFE

## Part Two · LOOKING THE PART

# PART ONE

*My Way of Life*

## ·I·

## A Point of View

Each September, in school, the teacher would say, "Write an essay on how you spent the summer."

Well, I've spent this summer writing this book, and doing a number of other things too. My home and my office are combined on a high floor of a Manhattan apartment house that has a cheerful California feeling about it, even in the winter. I get the first rays of the morning sun rising over the East River and, smog permitting, the last lovely colors of the sunset somewhere behind the Hudson. There are two small terraces where I try to keep some shrubbery going, and which my toy poodles adore, and I keep the rooms filled with plants and flowers. Even my dresses swarm with flowers.

I can see such big chunks of the sky that I know before the weather forecasters do whether my plane will be able to take off, if it's one of the many days of the year I'm leaving on another business trip. I have a bird's view of the world here, and a bird's sense of freedom. I have the same sense of excitement about the next adventure that I had when I was sixteen. And I'm sure I'll never lose it. All my nostalgia is for tomorrow—not for any yesterdays.

People are always asking me if there's anything I regret, or would change. The answer is no! Not a thing. If I hadn't had the pain I wouldn't be me. And I like being me. Everyone should. I have a friend who says, "Treasure yourself." I follow that advice by doing a certain amount of self-pampering. I surround myself with happy colors—yellow, coral, hot pink, and Mediterranean blues and greens. I've persuaded myself that I hate things that are bad for me—fattening food, late nights, and loud and aggressive people head the list. I'm friends with myself, so I do things that are good for me, otherwise I couldn't be good for others. I spend my time with people I'm fond of, and that includes my working time, too. Whether I'm at a board meeting or on a movie set I'm with good friends, so there's no drudgery about any of my jobs.

Not that I don't work hard. The demands I make on myself are fantastic. I expect perfection. I get it, at rare moments—but they're too rare.

Probably time is my only hangup. I organize myself right down to the second because I'm greedy. Greedy to fill every minute of my days with all the things I want to accomplish. And for the future I only want a small thing: a hundred years more to act, another hundred to learn to paint, a hundred to become a writer, and still another century to get a formal education.

Women are lucky, I think, because they can get so much more variety into their lives than most men can. With a little organization a woman can excel as wife, homemaker, mother, career woman, and gracious hostess, be lovely to look at and to be with —and still have time left over to be a good friend to a lot of people. And a *happy* friend. Of course, we all have our problems. But I don't inflict mine on my friends. At least I try not to.

How many people call you saying, "Oh, I woke up so tired this morning . . . I had such a terrible weekend . . . the day's awful outside." Being cheerful on the phone is part of giving. Sure, we all have our problems, but why inflict them on our friends? I think I can count on the fingers of one hand the people who call up with a cheery, happy voice—and keep it that way.

People with problems seem to find that telephone irresistible. When they're happy they just don't think about sharing it with other people.

Squeezing the most out of life takes a little executive planning. I used to say to the children when they were growing up, "If you have twelve things to do, and twelve hours to do them in, don't spend the first ten hours doing just one thing or you'll find yourself in an awful mess at the end of the day. *Plan.* And everything will get done."

George Bernard Shaw had another way of expressing it. "If you put off your work for thirty years," he said, "then you'll have to do thirty years' work in one day—and that will be a very bloody business indeed!" And I'd like to add that you'll miss thirty years of good living!

I am always on the set early. When they ask me why I say, "I'm afraid you'll start without me. Or replace me!" It used to be a Hollywood joke. But I never got over the idea that being on time was important. Not because I was so insecure, I think, but because I respect time, my own and other people's.

Today, after more than eighty-five pictures and dozens of television plays, I still rehearse everyone to death. I spend Saturdays and Sundays alone on the set, if necessary, going over and over my scenes. So that when we shoot, it's "Take One. Print!"

If I've driven myself it's been out of pure selfishness. I like to get up early in the morning because I can't wait for the day to begin. Before I go to bed at night, last thing, I make a little schedule for the next day. My secretaries, Florence Walsh in New York and Betty Barker in California, keep a schedule for about three months ahead—they have to keep retyping it as more and more things get packed into it. But getting each day's jobs done is *my* responsibility.

I get up, get through my shower and beauty routines, have a

simple breakfast, and fly to my desk. It doesn't take much time to commute from my kitchen to the room where I work, so I get a head start on a pile of mail. A package of it might have come in the night before from Betty Barker.

Betty started working for me on weekends way back in 1938, while she was working for Howard Hughes. I've been able to have her full time since 1955 and she's one of my dearest and most faithful friends. She holds down the fort in Hollywood, coping with all sorts of things, often without having to consult me. I dictate letters to her over the phone, or put them on a record for her to transcribe.

But whatever the source, yesterday's mail gets dealt with before I turn to today's. I don't like old business hanging over my head. When Florence arrives, promptly at nine, I'm ready to dictate replies and get started on my phone calls. Between the two of us we answer calls that come in on three lines. It can get pretty frantic.

A meeting's called at Pepsi-Cola—until recently only a seven-minute drive away. Now headquarters are sprawled out on a beautiful estate in Westchester. Public relations calls about six more bottling plants to be opened. We pencil in six more cities for the coming weeks. Some of them may be as far away as South America or the Middle East.

There's a film offer. I'll read the script tonight and if I like it I'll plan on two months in London in the fall. A good television show comes along. Yes, I can get out to the Coast the third week in September for the shooting. There are panel shows and talk shows that need a yes or no. I'm on the boards of a number of charities—perhaps fifteen. I try to attend their meetings, and every week I tape public-service announcements for some of them.

If I work at home all day I have a late lunch—and a light one

*Every morning that I'm in New York I'm at my desk with Florence promptly at nine.*

—and try to find twenty minutes to relax completely. There'll be a lot more work to finish before dinner.

On the rare evenings (and they're precious ones) that I can be at home alone, I'm America's number-one television fan. I travel so much, and spend so many evenings on a dais, that I'm always eager to catch up on my favorite shows. There are some that I never miss when I'm in New York, even if it means saying no, thank you, to a nice dinner invitation.

I do most of my moviegoing in front of my own television set—which was hilariously evident to the two friends who accompanied me to a private preview of *Trog*. It was ten-thirty in the morning, and I took along a six-pack of Pepsi. After we sat down I said, "We'll open three of these during the first commercial."

I have such a full schedule that it's hard for me to be flexible about seeing people at a moment's notice. For that reason I abhor dropper-inners. It happened to me recently. The house phone rang and the desk said that three people were on their way up. There I was at my desk, swamped with correspondence, wearing a little cotton shift and very little makeup.

I had to abandon everything, run quickly into my dressing room, get into a lovely dress I had bought in Canada, put on lipstick, and tidy my hair. I was furious. My own children wouldn't think of dropping in without calling to see if I'm busy. I wasn't rude. I said, "I'm sorry to have kept you waiting. I wasn't expecting guests." Fortunately, few people do this any more. I feel for women who are alone in a house when an unexpected and unwanted guest rings the doorbell.

This is my life today—a sketchy outline of it. In other years, when I was married, when I was raising children, when I was doing several films a year, the pattern was different but the quality has always been the same. Keeping busy, and cramming every bit of activity I possibly could into every hour.

If I have any one thing going for me, it's not that I'm Joan Crawford with a good job and a bank account, but the fact that I was born working. We had our ups and downs—more downs than ups. I helped my mother in the hand laundry she ran. Later I worked my way through two private schools washing dishes, cooking for the entire establishment, making beds, waiting on tables—and trying to get some studying done in between. But there was precious little time for books. I got to classes only two or three times a year.

In the second school I was the only helper in a fourteen-room house accommodating thirty other students and, in true Dickens fashion, I was thrown down the stairs and beaten with a broom handle. This should have turned me off housework forever, but the funny thing is that I still love scrubbing and ironing and especially cooking, and I could no sooner leave a bed unmade than I could fly to the moon. That school didn't teach me much out of books, but it certainly taught me to be self-sufficient, and I've never regretted it.

I do desperately regret not having had a formal education. I tried to make it at Stephens College, in Missouri, but I was completely unprepared, and when midterm exams loomed up I ran away. I knew I wouldn't be able to answer a single question. In the short time I was there, though, I made one of the dearest and most valuable friends I've ever had—the president of the college, Daddy Wood. He understood why I had to leave, but before I left he gave me three rules for living that may have helped me more than four years of the classics would have done. They're very precious to me:

1. Never quit a job until you finish it.

2. The world isn't interested in your problems. When your problems are the greatest, let your laughter be the merriest.

3. If you find you can do a job, let it alone, because you're bigger than the job already, and that means you will shrink down to its size. If the job is impossible, you may never get it accomplished, but you'll grow in *trying* to accomplish it.

In the years when I did three or four jobs at once it wasn't because of any compulsion to keep running till I dropped. It was because I loved all the jobs and wanted to be first-rate at every one of them. I loved being a good wife because making a man happy was the best working definition of happiness for *me*. Women have the privilege of being active and attractive in so many ways, and they should be glad, because inactivity is one of the great indignities of life. St. Thomas Aquinas said, "Why do you seek rest? You were only created to labor."

I still have a press clipping of an interview I gave when I was nineteen. I said then, "I want the Joan Crawford of this year to be only a building block for the Joan Crawford of next year. I never want to be second best. I haven't even begun to be what I want to be. I haven't done anything professionally with which I'm completely satisfied—although personally I have, as a woman."

Today I'd say the very same thing. I'm still geared for tomorrow. I know who I am, what I want to do, and where I want to go. And I've got a long way to go yet as far as my ambitions are concerned. I don't let myself get complacent. I've always pasted the bad notices on my mirror—and I read them before I perform.

I'm willing to tackle new things because I've never been afraid to ask: How is it done? Tell me everything about it. And then I work at it until I can do it as well as anybody else. If I'm lucky, better. Robert Gist, actor, director, and one of my close friends, maintains that I approach my work like a child—intuitively rather than intellectually. The magical thing about a child is its intuition, and he says I go back to that childlike state with each new job, each new challenge.

One of the first challenges I met when I started in pictures was, like a child's, to learn how to talk! I was born in San Antonio, and although I left there when I was a baby, something of Texas clung to my voice. They said I was the only girl in Hollywood who needed four syllables to say "yes." How I worked! I read out loud by the hour, whenever I was alone, until I could hear that it was coming right. Helen Hayes used the same technique with *her* southern accent.

Much later I gave myself an even bigger challenge. I adored music, and I wanted to do more than deliver little hotcha numbers in M-G-M musicals. While I was married to Franchot Tone I began studying seriously with Rosa Ponselle's coach, and when Rosa came to the Coast she and I sang duets together. Franchot too was studying opera and we had a glorious time with our arias from Verdi and Mozart. I had a three-octave range (I was a contralto) but there was a break in between the middle and third octaves that I never could overcome. Grand opera was a goal that I didn't attain, but I was the better for trying—proof of Daddy Wood's third rule. Anybody with a knowledge of voice knows that vocal training results in good voice projection—an invaluable asset for an actress. And incidentally it resulted in a rib cage that's a challenge to my dressmakers.

I've tried to meet challenges head on, and I've been lucky in learning how to overcome fears: by just jumping in. I used to be terrified of horses, so I bought a polo pony. I learned to mount the monster, to control him, and to feel confident. I was so proud of this achievement that I bought a second pony and played polo every chance I got. Then one day my pony suddenly took off down the field at supersonic speed. I lost my head and reined in, forgetting that you never rein in a polo pony, you guide him with your knees. Off we went, and I was helpless. A minute later a stallion came up a ramp. I couldn't see him, but my pony could, and he came to a dead stop. I went over his head in a triple somersault and landed right on my tail bone.

I got back on, but I thought—it isn't worth it. I'd conquered my fear, so what was I trying to achieve now? A broken neck? I didn't need that in my business, so I sold the ponies.

I used to be afraid of giving speeches to large groups of people. The first time I was on a podium I shook like an aspen. It was like amateur night. But somehow I got through it, and the second time was easier. Now it's a breeze—luckily, since I have a lot of public speaking to do in my job.

Perhaps the greatest fear I ever conquered was that of flying. In 1955 I'd never been in an airplane and I had no intention of ever climbing into one. But that was the year I became engaged to Alfred Steele, a man whose job as chairman of the board of Pepsi-Cola kept him airborne almost as much as he was on the ground. A huge wedding had been planned at the home of friends of ours in New Jersey. Six hundred guests had been invited. But a couple of days before, in Hollywood, Alfred turned to me at dinner and said, "Joan, let's fly to Vegas and get married tonight, quietly."

Panic caught me in the pit of my stomach. Fly? Me? And in that tiny plane of his? He didn't give me much time to think it over. He left the dinner table and phoned his pilot to tell him to warm up the plane. The next thing I knew I was at the airport. There was no turning back.

Alfred held me in his arms as we took off and kept talking, explaining what was happening.

"We're out of the traffic pattern now, twelve thousand feet, and climbing. The mountains are getting smaller."

He'd chosen a night when the flying was smooth as silk, but he explained how cloud formations can cause air pockets and turbulence that can make a plane bounce around. And how, no matter how much it bounced, we were perfectly safe. He knew so well that if I *understood* exactly what was happening I'd never be afraid again. And I wasn't. I've learned, as my friend advised, to treasure myself, but I still don't treasure the storms. And I've encountered a few in the several million air miles I've logged since that elopement to Las Vegas. But there's been a safe landing every time.

20

Conquering fears, whatever they may be, opens life up—and this life should be as full of different experiences as we can make it. Too many women build fences around themselves, especially as they grow older. They limit themselves, or feel that life has limited them.

"I'm just a housewife," they'll say, "I'm just a mother . . . and the kids are growing up. They don't need me any more. I'll settle down to my knitting now, and try to live with loneliness."

Well, I've known a lot of loneliness. Who hasn't? But I'll never settle down to my knitting and it. There are too damned many exciting things I haven't tried yet. And I'm planning to try quite a few of them!

# ·II·

# A Script for a Complete Woman

Everybody has strong ideas about marriage. And why not? It's the most intriguing situation a woman has in this life. It can be the most sublime, challenging, fulfilling, and precious one—the one that makes her a complete woman. Or it can be the most hellish. I sometimes wonder if men realize the power they have over us.

Not long ago I returned from a trip to Puerto Rico with Sharon Crane, the Pepsi PR girl who accompanied me for two years. We were so exhausted from all that heat and all the activity involved in the Variety Clubs International annual convention that we could hardly drag ourselves out of the plane and into our cars. All I wanted was bed. Oblivion.

I got home and suddenly the phone rang. A few minutes later I called Sharon.

"I don't feel tired at all any more," I announced in the most delighted, wide-awake tones. "Cary Grant just called me!"

It's that kind of thing. To hear that beautiful voice. Now if a man who's simply a very old and dear friend can have that effect on the phone, think what a husband can do! That's what I mean by the way a wonderful marriage makes a woman a *complete* woman—vital and alive.

We all think we have the formula for a good marriage—whether or not we've made it work ourselves—and I'm no exception. My recipe: Be a giver, not a taker. People talk about what they want out of marriage. They should think about what they have to put into it. It's worth every single bit of love and protection and unselfishness you can muster up. And believe me, you can muster up much more than you thought you could before you were married.

I've been married four times. Some people might say that anyone who's been married that often isn't meant for that state. Three failures—if they can be called that—are the most terrible, heartbreaking, anguishing experiences anyone can have. And they get worse each time. There is the awful feeling of insecurity—the asking, over and over, "What have I done wrong *this* time?"

But marriage, like everything else, is a learning experience, and I try to learn something from everything that happens, even if it hurts like hell.

I married Douglas Fairbanks, Jr., when we were both teenagers. Fun was the word for that one. We had a marvelous time. I tore into the business of housekeeping as if I'd invented it. I wanted to do everything myself, and I did it well. I sewed curtains, hooked rugs, knitted sweaters, and even made my own clothes so that there would be more to spend on the house. I took all kinds of lessons—French, Spanish, and music, and I read every book Doug mentioned. I worked like a demon to become a fine dramatic actress, and we played as if there were no tomorrow.

Doug taught me a lot of intangible things. To be more tolerant, to respect myself. Sometimes when I'd agonize over my early mistakes he'd say to me, "Billy, nothing you've ever done wrong is important at all if you've learned something for tomorrow."

I tried to give him confidence in his own talent, and the knowledge that he wasn't just riding along on a famous name. But he wasn't as ambitious as I was. He had a dozen talents and indulged them all in his easygoing way, but he'd never had to fight his way up the way I had, and he had no taste for it.

No, that marriage wasn't a failure. It ended because I took my work with deadly seriousness. How else can anyone succeed? I wanted Douglas, but I wanted work too, and the rest of the time with him. His interests were far-flung, and he loved having hordes of people around, throwing vast parties on the spur of the moment. I think he needed more outside stimulation than I did. No, I don't think it—I know it. We parted with deep sadness and mutual respect. And we're still lovely friends today, after so long.

After that divorce I saw Franchot Tone almost constantly because we had made several pictures together. Our friendship deepened until we had a very good thing going for us. I loved him. I adored his quiet self-assurance and his sophistication. I cherished every minute we spent together, but I was afraid. I'd been burned once, and I was pretty much convinced that two people bound up in similar careers should never marry. In fact, I had come to the conclusion that *I* should never marry again. At this point my career was demanding more and more of my time. Success was a beautiful thing, and I loved it. I was afraid that marriage would demand more than I could give to it.

It was Alfred Lunt and Lynn Fontanne who changed my mind. Not that they said anything. They're far too wise ever to give people advice about their personal lives. Just being with them and seeing how happy they were, and how their careers, rather than damaging their wonderful private relationship, had only enhanced it—that made me do some more thinking.

Lynn and Alfred were absolutely born for each other. He will start to tell a story and she'll finish it. Neither one of them ever tells a whole story by himself, or herself. But they never interrupt each other, either. They work together in private life as they do in the theater, even in their own home, complementing, never upstaging the other.

Observing them, I capitulated. Franchot and I were married.

Franchot was a beautiful person and a very courageous one, as Burgess Meredith pointed out at his funeral. "He was endowed," as Buzz said, "with many graces, and with a deep love of nature that I shared."

We both worked hard at building a life together that was completely apart from our acting, and to a large extent we succeeded. We only gave small dinner parties on Saturday nights for our closest friends, and occasionally had a buffet for forty or fifty people in the garden. We were so much less social than most of Hollywood those days that columnists made teasing remarks about our being "in retreat." Nevertheless it was careers that came between us, finally. Does this always have to be the case in Hollywood?

There wasn't the slightest doubt in my mind that Franchot was by far the finer actor, but he was only getting "good" parts. I was getting stardom. The star system at Metro was in full sway and I was one of Mr. Mayer's fair-haired girls. I got the juiciest parts and the biggest build-ups—not to mention the highest salaries. Franchot's roles, especially in my pictures, were secondary ones. There was nothing I could do about it. One writer said, "Sensitive husbands don't like second billing." Franchot was sensitive —very sensitive.

If that marriage was a failure, the failure was mine. I've said that one must give. Perhaps I should have given up my career entirely. But I felt I was born to be an actress and I'd worked so hard to achieve what I had! I'd had the taste of success, and it was very palatable. I just couldn't give it up. I've never changed. Even now, I just can't wait for the next *good* script to come in.

Perhaps if my story were put in the proper perspective it might be one of many lonely years punctuated by attempts to find an outlet for all the love I've had to give. I had my blessed children to come home to, but they couldn't fill *all* of the void. When I tucked them into bed I'd wonder why it had turned out like this.

Believe me, it was not self-pity, ever. I was searching for the answer; wanting a real marriage, and being so much alone. This was my only excuse for marrying Phillip Terry, a quiet, reserved man who wanted the same kind of simple home life that I did. He brought me peace of mind and companionship—and I persuaded myself that it was love. It wasn't. That was my fault from beginning to end.

There was a famous joke about the beginning, though. After I divorced Franchot I asked my maid to unpick all the "T's" in my linens—acres of towels, meadows of bed linens. I don't know how many hundreds of "T's" the poor girl had carefully unpicked when, one evening, listening to the radio, she heard the announcer break in with a news bulletin: *Joan Crawford has just married Phillip Terry!*

The maid threw down the pillowcase she was working on and screamed, "I quit!"

For ten years I was alone, I filled the days with work, with the children, and with a few good friends. And I made a friend of myself. To have a friend you have to be one. You have to learn to like yourself—which usually means getting over a few bad habits. I'm sure that I grew a little wiser, and I learned something about faith. Instead of being frantic about having to cope with life by myself I decided that God probably knew what He was doing and would solve things in His own good time. And that's the way it was.

Hollywood gave me a wonderful career. Maybe I was the one who gave myself three unhappy endings and untold loneliness. But never bitterness. That word isn't in my working vocabulary. I'm the sum of everything that's ever happened to me, of every mistake I've made and every tear I've shed—although I made sure there weren't many of those. And I tried never to *repeat* a mistake. After a catastrophe I take a deep breath, pin on a grin, and get on with something else. I say, Okay, I did the wrong thing. What did I learn from *that?* I'll never do it again! But no experience I've ever had has made me bitter—nor ever will.

I've seen what it does to too many people. When one lives with bitterness it always shows in the face, and it's pathetic. The mouth is beat. The softness goes out of the eyes. The body is stooped. Bitterness and self-pity are deadly poisons that can't be hidden. They seem to exude from the pores.

Thank God I've never allowed myself time for either one, and I owe it to my natural view of the world. I love it. I want to live, to love and be loved—to give everything I can. And you can't be a giver if you're bitter.

The English writer and critic V. S. Pritchett wrote recently: "Love is always too early but never too late." What a wonderful line. And how well it applies to me—and perhaps to you. I achieved, at last, a completely happy marriage, and I think it was those early difficult periods that made it possible. It needed a wonderful, mature man, too. But that man probably wouldn't have fallen in love with the earlier Joan Crawford who still had so much learning to do.

When I met Alfred Steele I had become the kind of woman a man like that could fall in love with. For that I'll never stop being thankful.

When we were married I'm sure he didn't expect me to take an avid interest in the soft-drink business. His true-blue friends said he'd married a movie star. He probably thought that one of the conditions of this marriage would be having to file his problems at the office and come home to a pampered woman full of Hollywood gossip or accounts of what the children had been up to. The twins, Cathy and Cindy, were only nine at that time. And this was a man who slept, ate, *lived* his job. It was his baby.

From the very beginning he got a surprise that bowled him over. I was fascinated by his work. And when he saw that I was so eager and hungry to know all about it he was enchanted. I asked questions all the time we traveled—and we traveled a great deal overseas when we were first married. Who are the people we're going to meet? What are they like? What role do they play in the business? What are your plans for this area? I wanted to go with him to see the new plants and how they operated.

"But you don't have to, darling," he said at first.

"But I want to," I assured him. And I really did.

It was a marvelous feeling to work with him and to feel that I was learning *his* way of life, and helping him. And it meant so very much to him. He couldn't have been happier. From the beginning of our marriage, his company became *our* child. We stimulated each other, out of mutual love and pride.

Those trips are among my most exciting memories. We went to Beirut, the Belgian Congo, Uganda, Kenya, Zanzibar, Mexico, and dozens of places across the United States. Each was different. Each was a beautiful new experience. Africa was, in a sense, my baptism in Pepsi, and I have a great affection for that continent.

I remember, on that first trip, we arrived in Portuguese East Africa at seven in the morning. As we were approaching for a landing I said, "I can't put on any makeup, Alfred. It's just too hot. And nobody's going to be there anyway. They don't know me here."

As we taxied in I saw in amazement that there were twenty thousand people in that little airport. "Who's on board?" I asked. "Who are they waiting for?"

He grinned. "You, darling!"

*Our first big trip for Pepsi was to Africa.*

And it was true. My pictures have found their way to the most remote corners of the world. It's the most wonderful, enchanting thing. I came down the ramp and one little girl, about ten or eleven years old, reached up to me and I kissed her and left some lipstick on her cheek. Then they all wanted the same thing. I gave them every lipstick I had with me—but I couldn't kiss twenty thousand people! As I moved through the crowd they kept kissing my hands and arms, just wanting to touch me.

And never a language barrier. I could learn to say "thank you" in almost every language I happened to need. And my name is an easy one to pronounce—everywhere except in Italy, where it's "Jon Croff."

A lovely house was reserved for us in Leopoldville, complete with French chef. We visited native villages and were fascinated with their art work and enchanted by their music. Above, a village in Zululand.

Zululand was fantastically colorful and the friendliest place ever.

My Way of Life

During the African tour we spent a night at Treetops, that famous hotel built high in the trees in the middle of a game preserve where Elizabeth II was staying when she learned that she had become Queen of England. Way out there in the wilderness, it's one of the most luxurious places in the world. The food can compete with that of "21" in New York.

We started out early in the morning because everyone has to be up top by two-thirty in the afternoon. Before we climbed up I walked around with a white hunter, scattering coarse salt to attract the elephants, because a herd hadn't been seen in seven days. I also noticed that a ladder was attached to about every fourth tree. The white hunter said they were for safety: "If you hear any sound, run to the first ladder and *climb!*" I shivered. I couldn't hear a thing, but I saw some tracks and asked him what they were. "Elephant tracks," he said. "And fresh ones."

"Let's get going," I gulped, and shot straight up to the hotel in the sky. We weren't completely free of wild companionship even there. Baboons would scramble up to take a look at us and chatter. But they were tame, and people fed and petted them.

From two-thirty until dusk we had to talk in whispers. Small sounds carry for miles out there, and most of the jungle beasts have acute hearing. We didn't want to frighten them away. At sundown even our whispers had to stop. We removed our shoes and walked quietly in bare feet. We crowded to the windows and waited while a simulated moonlight controlled by a rheostat very gradually grew brighter. Then, to our delight, two huge herds of elephants emerged and made their way to the water hole, walking so delicately with their great feet that hardly a twig snapped. The bulls led the way. Babies trotted along underneath their mothers and when one of them ran ahead the bull would bat it back to safety with his trunk.

It was an awesome sight as we sat there in candlelight, almost holding our breath.

Overnight at Treetops was an exciting break in the trip—a luxurious hotel perched in the trees in a game preserve in Kenya. I got up the courage to go down and toss out crude salt for the elephants, and later tame baboons came all the way up to the top to greet us.

We were always interested in the paintings and sculpture in Africa and bought quite a few things. We were lucky that our Belgian Congo bottler, Maurice Alhedeff, owned an atelier that turned out art objects in a variety of media. While we were looking around, a little boy of about eleven came in and Maurice asked him, in Swahili, what he would like to do. Painting? Ceramics? The little boy said that his life's ambition was to carve from ivory.

Maurice led us all into another room and pointed to an elephant's tusk that must have been one of the biggest ever taken from one of those splendid animals and that to the little boy must have looked the size of a tree—and that big around. His eyes widened, his mouth fell open, and we could see him frantically thinking, "Where do I start?" Maurice laughed, turned to a boy of about sixteen, and said, "Get your last piece of work."

It was brought in—a small, delicate carving. The little boy nodded. "This is what I want to do." And then in Swahili the boy asked, "But where do I start on this great big tusk?" The older apprentice said, "I'll show you." That's how it starts. One trains the other, down through the generations. Maurice brings dozens of these boys in from the bush every year and trains them so that they'll always have a good livelihood.

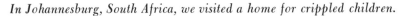

*In Johannesburg, South Africa, we visited a home for crippled children.*

*A warm welcome at Government House in Uganda.*

When traveling in Africa it's protocol to first check into Government House before going to your hotel—even if it's six in the morning, as it was when we arrived in Uganda. It was incredibly hot (this is the only part of traveling that I dislike) and I was assured that we only needed to sign the register. But then it seemed that King Frederick, the Kabaka of Uganda, had got up early in order to meet us, and we were to have an audience.

King Frederick asked us to be seated—and to my astonishment, he knew every part I'd ever played in a film and asked me all about them. Then he wanted to know everything about the Pepsi-Cola business. He was completely charming. I forgot how hot and tired we were and the time flew. What was supposed to have been a three-minute audience ran to an hour and ten minutes, and we enjoyed every bit of it.

Some of my memories are not so beautiful. I remember a large formal luncheon when two bugs plopped themselves into my *petite marmite.* I asked the waiter to take it back—but the lady sitting opposite told me not to bother: "If your soup goes back to the kitchen the same bowl will come back with even more bugs in it. You're going to be eating them all the time here." I told myself that all these people ate them and they looked very healthy. But I just stirred the bugs around politely and skipped the soup.

We took a house there with a staff, including a French chef— though when we entertained I was never entirely sure what would appear on the table because my French wasn't very reliable. We were well protected in that house. A six-foot-seven-inch-tall man slept on the hard floor of the balcony outside our living-room window, in case a wild animal tried to pay a visit. We never had to worry about his sleeping too soundly. At the slightest sound those men were on their feet in a split second. Their senses are so keen they can hear the falling of a leaf from a tree.

One year we managed to take all four children abroad and we settled for a time in Switzerland. Since this is the heart of Europe it meant that Alfred could take quick day-long trips to half a dozen other countries on business, or invite his associates to our hotel there for conferences. This was a working vacation for him. I organized it so that I had time for all four children, and for my husband too.

My days belonged to the children. We had different hours for different things. The older ones went skiing. The twins were frightened of the steep slopes so they went ice skating in the morning and had their naps in the afternoon. How they fought those naps! But I made them lie down—I darkened the room, and that was that. Usually they'd drop off pretty quickly, more sleepy from that Alpine air than they thought they were. I sat with them while they ate an early supper, bathed them, heard their prayers, and tucked them in. Then it was my husband's turn to have my complete attention.

*Four children and two dogs accompanied us for a long stay at St. Moritz.
This was Cathy.*

*We skied and skated.*

41

*I acquired a knitting machine and had a ball with it when I got home.*

*During Christmas week in St. Moritz a white beribboned piglet was a feature of the ceremonies.*

*Driving from Paris to Le Havre to board our ship we spent the night at a lovely auberge.*

During the most blissful years of my life the dead center of my life was my husband. I worked with him, and I made sure that he was as comfortable and happy as a man could, and should, be. Our home was designed to please him, and I was delighted when he wanted to bring his work back to it and share it with me. I organized his quiet times and made sure that children had been taken care of and that phones and doorbells wouldn't disturb him while he had some well-earned relaxation. Meals could always be produced on short notice for any number of people because I planned a week in advance—or tried to, but there were always extra meetings, extra people. Maybe the most important thing was that *I* was planned in advance. When he came home I was well groomed, fragrant, feminine. He never saw a laundry bag, a dust cloth, or a hair curler. I hope he never knew that such things existed!

On our Mexican trip it was for-
malities, fun, and fishing.

44

## A Script for a Complete Woman

Alfred was simply delighted when I encouraged him to bring his work home with him. In fact I insisted on it so that I could be sure he wasn't overtiring himself.

I used to say to him, "You must leave the office at four. Come back here and have your tea, or a cup of hot soup."

We used to love a cup of turtle soup at that time of day. It's a comforting brew, and very nourishing. Then I'd insist that he rest—put up his feet and completely relax.

This was *his* quiet time. The children had been fed (I wouldn't let any tired businessman go through that rat race) and they were told to man the telephone and the doorbell and make sure that he wasn't disturbed. Later he'd see them and ask them what they'd done during the day, and encourage them to express their opinions. That hour was a lovely one. Then off they went—the oldest to do their homework, the babies to bed.

Often Alfred's meetings began again at six. Two or more business associates would come and closet themselves in the study for almost an hour. Sometimes I'd join them, bringing in a tea tray and a few things to munch on—because no man with low blood sugar ever comes to a happy agreement about anything. With either tea or cocktails I like to give a busy man something hearty, like slices of salami or sausage. Or peanut butter and bacon on black bread slipped under the grill until it sizzles.

Another meeting might be scheduled the same night for seven. That group would be received in the living room and offered a drink and something to nibble on until Alfred was free to join them. I never knew whether those attending the seven o'clock meeting would stay for dinner, but I always had to be prepared. That's why I haven't had a cook for eighteen years. What cook can go on being cheerful if you tell her at a quarter to eight that there are going to be five extra people for dinner when she, after putting in a long day, has planned on two lamb chops? Besides,

45

I loved being alone with my husband when it was possible. So we had only one maid in our New York apartment, and I still have only one in my present eight rooms. Once a week we have men to come in and move the heavy furniture and do all the heavy cleaning and polishing—twice a week if I entertain much. The rest of the time my maid Mamacita and the faithful Mr. Grant and I manage very well by ourselves.

The difference between a hired cook and me was that when I was married I did the job for love—and enjoyed every minute of it. My freezer was always filled with things for emergencies, things like pot roast, beef bourguignon, lobster Newburg, creamed chicken, and meat loaf. I always made extra sauce so that the meat or chicken or seafood was completely covered when it was frozen. That's important. I kept frozen aspics and, of course, those lovely homemade soups that I cooked in great quantities and froze in separate containers. Apart from the soups, which simmer for hours, things should always be a little undercooked because they'll cook a bit more in the thawing and warming-up process.

At those rare times when no hearty dish was on tap I phoned Casserole Kitchen, a gem of a place that would send over a casserole of veal or lamb, or whatever, vegetables and salad, bread, and desserts. I'd have the oven ready and just pop things in for warming. I always had my own French dressing, and fruit and cheese in the refrigerator.

The point of all this planning was that when it was my husband's time of day I was prepared for almost any eventuality, for anything that he wanted to do. There might be a dozen unexpected guests, or a candlelit dinner for two—and we *always* dined by candlelight. When we were alone, if he wanted to talk business, so did I. I was interested, and he knew it. I never regaled him with an account of what the children had done, the lateness of deliveries because of traffic, or the neighborhood gossip (unless it was a particularly juicy bit!). There's nothing less stimulating for a man than the day-to-day business of raising four children. That's woman's work. If she's lucky she revels in it. If not, she gets it done anyhow, and in the time allotted for it.

Such a pattern of living calls for the same kind of executive ability a man has to develop in his office. It's not easy. It's not easy at all to run a house—small or, as in my case, large as it was then—give the children all the attention they should have, adjust to day-to-day crises, and be cool, collected, and captivating at six o'clock. Not only must the children and the housekeeping be dealt with and finished, the wife should also emerge at that hour "finished"— in the sense that she has all her beauty treatments behind her and is groomed, fragrant, and looking ready for an evening with her favorite beau.

A busy housewife might ask, but why *should* I go to all this trouble for the guy? To me, and to other women I've talked to, the answer's simple: You love him and you want to please him, make him happy. Love can spring out of a need for security—not financial security, but the security of being wanted, adored. That's why women can give so much. When we're needed we become dynamos, and we're always looking for ways to please, do something special, serve something the man loves that we can't afford, that he only gets at an occasional party on a canapé.

People will say they're not Joan Crawford and can't afford trainloads of caviar. Well, Joan Crawford can't either, but that's beside the point. If it's his birthday and he loves caviar, skip the hairdresser a couple of times. Give up a hat that you don't need. You'll find that you won't be giving *up* anything at all. You'll have the joy of giving *to*.

Surprise him, make him happy, and keep him interested, intrigued by you. You have to be attractive, sexy, to him. If every woman could walk into her husband's office and see how many beautiful women pass his desk every day it would give her something to think about. Which woman does *she* want to be like? I don't mean that she should go in there and stand around making him nervous while he's trying to work, or make him take her to lunch. But she could find some excuse just to drop in and observe what her husband is exposed to every day.

Being the woman he most enjoys going to bed with isn't quite enough—or won't be, for long. Sex is very beautiful, very personal, magnificent. But like all marvelous things she should come in a lovely wrapping. Have you ever opened a Christmas present that was wrapped with old brown paper and tied with string? Not even wrapped as a gift? You think, Good grief, they stepped on this, or sat on it, before sending it! The person who sent it didn't bother to take the time or trouble to make a nice presentation. Packaging is very important. How can any woman present *herself* in a careless package?

Each man has his own idea of what is "sexy." It's not necessarily long trailing negligees and see-through things. Alfred adored me without makeup, except for a little lipstick, and in something simple like a little cotton dress. I had to dress up for so many occasions—when we traveled, or when associates came to our home—and of course he wanted me to. But he liked to have a different Joan for himself. When we were alone I'd scrub off all the makeup until my face was shining, slip into something completely simple and comfortable, and it made a nice change for him. And it was exciting change!

I remember one day when we were on the beach in Jamaica; I was coming in out of the sea when a wave hit me. I'd had my back turned to the sea, which one should never do. I toppled over and came up, breathless, and with salt water running all down my hair and face and body.

Alfred came out to meet me, took my face in his hands and

kissed me and said, "You're the most beautiful thing I ever saw in my life!" I knew then what he loved in me. That was his very private Joan.

Females are born flirts. I've watched my three girls flirting almost from the time they were able to get their eyes opened and they could focus. They cooed at men, fluttered around them—and flattered them. But once girls get themselves married they forget the romance—and that's when the flirting should really begin. If you want to keep your husband, that is. A lot of other women are flirting with him and flattering him—you can depend on that.

A woman should tease her husband. Of course he's moody at times. Downright impossible, in fact. Who isn't? We are too. But you can't live in this world without a sense of humor. Tease each other out of grouchy moods. Never use sarcasm. If he's moody, you get brighter. If he's already bright you can indulge your own moods, because then he's in a position to take it.

This should start at the beginning of a marriage, though. If you start suddenly, after a few years, he'll get a shock. He'll say, what's happened to her? She's too happy! What's she *doing* with her afternoons? She's got a fella! So work into this gradually.

There should always be a precious time together at the end of the working day. Turn off the phone, ignore the door, pour a glass of wine or fruit juice. Shed the world and learn about each other in your own romantic oasis.

Of course none of us can really acquire a new personality, but we can improve on what we've got. In the most important ways I'm the same person I was at fourteen when I got my first Broadway job, or did my first jazz movies, or won my Oscar for my role in *Mildred Pierce*. I know I have the same eagerness, the same enormous curiosity, and the same optimism. But I'm told by someone who's known me practically from the beginning that I'm a constant source of surprise—that people are never sure what I'm going to do next, what I'm going to look like, or even what voice I'm going to use.

Maybe that's partly the actress in me. Maybe it's because I just won't take myself for granted. If a woman starts taking herself for granted, or taking her husband for granted, she's asking for trouble. And the remedy must start with the wife. She must take a sharp look at herself and, if necessary, edit herself.

She should sit down and inspect the contents of her head. What has she got to talk about tonight? Did she read an interesting article, go to a good lecture, get the background on an important news story, or glance through the business pages to see how *her* husband's industry is doing? I think that last activity might be the most important.

I know a woman whose husband is an expert in electronics. Her knowledge of the subject used to be limited to knowing how to change a light bulb, and she wasn't completely sure about that—like James Thurber's grandmother, she had a secret conviction that when the socket was empty the electricity ran out all over the table.

But she realized, while her babies were still toddlers, that she was totally engrossed in them, and that her husband was being made to take a back seat. And that he might not feel like occupying it alone for very long. He was getting ahead rapidly as an electrical engineer and he loved talking about it; if he couldn't talk to *her*, she realized, he just might find someone else.

So she wheeled her babies over to the public library and started at the beginning, reading about electricity from a textbook. And she got her husband to help her with her homework. He was enchanted. What's more, she became really interested in the subject. She organized her chores and the babies' routines so that she had several hours a day to study, and she was ready to talk shop whenever her husband was. She'll never be on his level, of course, but she's learning enough to ask really intelligent questions about his day's work, and to understand, when he comes home bubbling with a new achievement, what it's all about. This gal has done a very smart thing, in my book.

Make your husband talk about his work. *Drag* it out of him, if you have to. But, you're saying, my husband's a cashier. How can I take an interest in that? Well, for openers, you might say, "Any holdups today?" And go on to find out what keeping books is all about. What an auditor is. Follow changes in tax laws in the daily newspaper. You might even find all this fascinating. *He* has to.

I think it's important to make friends of your husband's business associates, too. They're a very important part of his life—in fact he probably sees more of them than of his family, and he necessarily becomes involved with them on a personal level. In encouraging my husband to bring his meetings home—and in taking a small part in the discussions myself—I made close friends not only with his associates but with their wives. I think that I was able to interest them still more in the business.

When we first went on tours for Pepsi I always attended the early morning meetings, but I found that the other women went shopping. Then the husbands would say, "Joan was at the meeting all morning."

The wives would ask, "What was she wearing?"

Soon they began coming themselves. In the beginning it might have been just to see what I was wearing. But they stayed, and became interested in the discussions, and were able to talk intelligently with their husbands about their problems.

Of course many women can't attend such meetings, or meet the people their husbands work with. But there are always the office parties, and wives should make a point of attending them, reaching out to the people they meet there, and forming new friendships. As for the boss, it would be a good thing to go up to him and thank him for being so nice to your husband. After you leave he'll probably say, "What a charming woman! Who's her husband?" And he'll be nice from then on in, even if he wasn't before. That's being protective. It's being involved. And if *you* don't get involved in his interests, someone else will.

This doesn't apply only to business. A man may be a fiend for baseball, football, or poker. A smart woman makes a real effort to find out what goes on at second base or on the ten-yard line, and she should know better than to draw to an inside straight. Many men like to share hobbies as long as their wives aren't complete idiots and ask, "Why is that man running?"

Of course the other side of this coin is that many men like to cultivate hobbies that give them a chance to get off *alone*— gardening, stamp collecting, building something in the basement, for example. And that's a cue to let him have his privacy. Just find out whether he wants to share an interest with you or go off like Walter Mitty and have extravagant daydreams in the carrot patch.

Play it by ear. If he wants to talk about the home run, get a book and find out the rules of the game. Or take some golf lessons. You don't have to be a pro to get around an eighteen-hole course with him. You have a lovely healthy afternoon together outdoors and then you can share the relaxation at the Nineteenth Hole. Some old friends of mine, the Ardmores, learned to play together. But even if your husband is already an expert go out and start learning. Surprise him. Wait until you're very good and then say, "How about a foursome?"

He'll think, Oh God, no! And then, play your B-movie scene —stand up and drive one straight down the fairway. A wife knows how best to impress her husband. If she doesn't, she'd better start learning.

The most "together" couple I know, Florence and J. Lincoln Morris, who is my lawyer, were childhood sweethearts. While he was in law school she studied to become a legal secretary, so that she could be his. They've not only worked together, they enjoy all the same amusements, all the same sports, and they've developed a unique and sensible system of taking lots of little vacations together. They've seen too many men work themselves to death, literally. So they decided to work for three weeks and then head out for a ten day cruise. They can afford it now, and they've earned it. And they love each other's company so much that they never get bored.

Alfred promised me that he would do just that—work for four weeks and on the fifth take a complete rest. That's the only way to arrange it because a man who's deeply involved can't shorten his work day very easily but he *can* organize a complete break. Unhappily, Alfred didn't do this. That's why he died.

I've been married to three actors, and since we shared a profession there was no disparity of interests. But each of them brought me more than shop talk. I have been fortunate enough to marry men who were well educated, cultivated, with a love of good literature, good music, all the fine arts. Since my own formal education was brief and sketchy I was avid to be introduced to the world of great works. With Douglas I read Shakespeare. With Franchot I studied it, worked through the parts, playing scenes with him.

I read voraciously. If a book or author was mentioned I bought it the next day and plunged in, prepared or not, to unravel the mysteries of Nietzsche, Dostoevski, or Proust, usually mispronouncing the names at the start. Words fascinated me—they still do. I had a little trick. I'd open my dictionary in the morning at random, pick an intriguing word, find the meaning, and use it as often as I could that day. By evening it was mine for keeps.

Douglas, who had been educated in Europe, had a fine talent for art, and wonderful taste. He sculpted and painted in our garden, and taught me how to look at art works and understand them. I was fortunate. My own taste developed and I learned to be more selective in my viewing and buying. I learned to value my own opinions. And that, in the end, is the real purpose of education. To know what to look for, where to find it, and how to judge it.

I don't think education should ever stop, either for a man or for a woman. When learning stops, vegetation sets in. I have the most tremendous respect for one of my business associates, Bob Kelly, who went back to graduate school after he'd become well established in his career. He was married and had three children and a very demanding job. But for several years he attended evening classes, commuting for an hour and a half after that to get home. He acquired both his master's and his doctorate. His wife had some lonely times, but she was behind him a hundred percent.

There's another couple I admire and love who made even greater sacrifices—Jane and Tom Sugars. Alfred Steele established a graduate scholarship at his own school, Northwestern University, and Tom Sugars won it in 1962. He won it on the basis of an excellent academic record at Southern Methodist University, and *that* had been an impressive achievement for both him and Jane—he was thirty-two years old when they decided that he should try for a college education. They had two small children and no money, but Jane was able to give music and voice lessons. She kept their home in Wichita Falls going, took care of the children, and contributed something toward his expenses.

At S.M.U. Tom took a part-time job that earned his room and

board. He and Jane were a hundred and fifty miles apart, and could only manage to visit each other every three weeks. Tom was thirty-five when he won the Steele Scholarship, and during that year, when he earned his graduate degree in marketing, family life began to become a memory. It was a thousand-mile trip and they only managed three weekends. But, as Jane says, they packed a lot of wonderful living into those three visits! Tom now has an important executive job which would never have been possible if he'd decided, in his thirties, that he was "too old" for an education.

Daddy Wood of Stephens College, where I spent much too short a time, kept in touch with me all his life, until he died at the age of eighty-eight. For most of his rich career he cherished the idea that women in their early forties were all longing to take up their schooling again. Many hadn't finished high school, others had never gone to college. At forty they suddenly found time on their hands and the feeling that they'd fallen behind their husbands and children intellectually.

He took a survey and discovered that his guess was absolutely right. He checked with all the Stephens students of his lifetime and also took a poll from other housewives. The response of both groups was fantastic. Ninety-nine percent of them wanted to go back to school!

But how many of them, I wonder, followed through and actually started attending classes again? Reading on your own isn't enough. We're most of us too lazy. There's something essential about the discipline of having to get to the school, compete with other students, and meet the challenge of examinations. Finally there's the wonderful satisfaction of receiving a diploma, a certificate, or a degree.

In many marriages it can be the woman's privilege to bring new interests into her husband's life. A man can become completely absorbed in business, or he may have had to neglect other things in the struggle to get ahead. Get him interested in the new book you've brought home—a good one! Hang some good reproductions on the walls or, if your taste is sure, find interesting originals. Buy some good recordings and just let them seep in. Grown men don't like the feeling that they're being taught, but things can filter in. Finally, enjoying something first-rate together is the most satisfying experience anyone can have—be it sex or a symphony, it's good and it's shared.

A wife who lets herself deteriorate into a concubine, completely dependent on her husband for her sense of life, not only makes him feel guilty, she becomes the world's worst bore. An educated woman means an educated family. She sparks the children because she has a range of interests and a curious mind that wants to go on learning.

# ·III·

# Setting the Stage

Love NEEDS the most beautiful setting that it can get. A few
great pieces of theater have been mounted on bare stages—*Our
Town, Don Juan in Hell,* and the one-man performances of John
Gielgud, to name a few that come to mind. But lacking a pro-
scenium arch, a good marriage deserves a lovely background. And
a lovely background requires taste, and all the professional help
you can get.

My own decorating experiments have run the gamut of style—I
can hardly remember all the things I've tried. In one of my first
houses, a rented one, I had portraits of dancing girls done in
black velvet with blond hair (real hair!) and rhinestones and
pearls (not real). I guess they were typical of the twenties. I
thought them beautiful. Paul Bern, one of my guiding lights and
best friends, came to pick me up one night, gazed at my "art"
display, and gulped. I got rid of them fast.

After that William Haines took over my decorating. He still
loves to tell the story of those black-velvet girls, and he very tact-
fully began steering me in new directions. Not that it was all tact
and harmony. We'd fight like cats and dogs over some of his ideas.
He always won because of his excellent taste and knowledge and
my lack of both. The first house he did for me was in what he
describes as Ming Toy cocktail Chinese, and then we went

through periods the way some women go through wardrobes. I'm moody, and I like change. I'm impatient too, and like it to be instant change. Of course that never happened. I could storm around and bite my nails and climb the walls, but it takes time to acquire good things, find the right places for them, create perfect atmospheres. After the "cocktail Chinese" we went on to Americana. That must have been the time when I was hooking my own rugs and there were little rocking chairs all over the place for the children. But it didn't feel like me.

There was a baroque phase, and then came eighteenth-century English. Billy found me some beautiful antique pieces—in wood that had been lovingly polished for two hundred years. I never could stand the traditional English couches, though. They were so straight, always catching you in the wrong place in the back. So I said, "Why can't we put in modern couches and comfortable chairs?" He said, "No reason." So he designed the most beautiful comfortable couches with deep soft cushions that you could curl up and get lost in.

I had snow-white carpets that made a stunning background for the piecrust tables and other antique pieces. There were corner cabinets, all chiseled out and hand carved, painted a lovely pale pink to show off my collection of Wedgwood and Chinese things. I had the Wedgwood in green, black, pink, and the traditional light blue. The walls we painted in what Billy calls the Crawford blue, a little lighter than Wedgwood . . . soft, soft. It was the most beautiful, romantic room to walk into.

The children's rooms were very modern, with happy wallpaper and all the drawer space they could possibly need. Christopher liked to have his friends over to spend the night, so I gave him my beautiful library paneled in Philippine pine and had two bunk beds put in.

Christina, my oldest daughter, inherited the first real bed I had ever bought myself—after a dreary procession of Murphy beds in

the struggling days. It was an antique four-poster canopied bed that Billy found for me. I replaced all the fabric and made a bedspread to match the canopy and it was Christina's after she grew out of the baby-pink nursery and the "sleep-safes," those bands that keep a baby safely in bed. And as I said, there were little rocking chairs for each of them until they were too old to fit into them.

We often slept in the garden, by the pool or in the theater. The theater, which was beside the pool, had an enormous fireplace. I

*There was a lot of space behind my house in Brentwood, California, and we spent a lot of our time there enjoying the theater, the badminton court, and the pool with its bathhouses. This is Christina, my eldest daughter.*

kept as many as eighteen sleeping bags in the house and in the wintertime we'd all go there—the children and as many friends as they wanted to invite—with a massive supply of popcorn and marshmallows. We'd move back all the furniture and stretch out in front of the fire all night.

In summer we'd sleep around the swimming pool. I always took the diving board (not the part with the water underneath it!) and we'd start out on top of our sleeping bags. But by three or four in the morning, even during a California summer, it would get chilly and we'd crawl inside. We had plenty of fruit and milk and snacks and the kids would tell stories and giggle until the soft peace of the night enveloped them. Gradually the stillness and darkness would take over, and tired from swimming, they'd all drift off.

In good weather the big outdoors area became part of the house, and vice versa. When the living-room walls were tinted a pale pink I added apple-green accents and the combination was breathtaking when the sun poured in. It was like being in an apple orchard in full bloom. Dark rooms, to me, are very depressing.

During the English period I found some new Chinese things— but this time the right things, fine old pieces instead of the cocktail variety: beautiful porcelain, china, and the loveliest Georgian silver, all collected little by little as I could afford it.

I wasn't the easiest client in the world. Billy wanted chintz, but I was determined not to have it in my living room. I'd learned that lesson. I think the first gay, happy things I ever bought for myself were chintz curtains. But the place got so damned busy that it made me dizzy—too many patterns have the same effect on me as those very tiny mosaic tiles you sometimes see in public places, especially in airports. Judy Garland used to get so seasick looking at them that she had to be carried out of the area with her eyes shut tight.

## Setting the Stage

Billy helped me with the home Alfred Steele and I created in New York. It was a very special place, occupying the top two floors and overlooking Central Park. Originally it had eighteen rooms. We broke them down into eight large ones, with huge windows. I wanted to bring a California ambiance with me so we picked bright colors and built in lots of the conveniences that aren't so common in the older buildings in New York. There was a marvelous free-flying staircase, and the wall alongside it was punctuated with large green plants. At the top was a skylight. Sunlight permeated the whole apartment and was refracted by the white carpet. Even the room we called the office was in light, gay colors. There wasn't a dark nook in the whole place— except possibly the broom closet.

*The staircase leading to the bedroom floor.*

*View of the living room in the penthouse we rebuilt and decorated on Fifth Avenue.*

There were large raised fireplaces in the drawing room and bedroom, and a working fountain in the two-level bedroom. Curtains, draperies, and upholstery were all hand woven.

Billy says that most women perfunctorily consult their husbands when they're decorating, and then go ahead and do what they want—and that the man usually ends up with a dark closet for his living quarters.

When Alfred and I started planning the Fifth Avenue apartment he said, "You just go ahead. After all, it's your home."

"No," I said. "It's *our* home. I want you to be happy in every room. I don't want you to go from one room to another unhappy with one single piece of furniture, or one color."

So he was consulted about every item. Every piece of furniture was made to order for its special place. He wanted a bright green carpet for his study, and agreed with me on pink for our bedroom. How I adore pink!

Usually there's no great clash in taste between a couple. After all, he saw her in her own setting before he decided to marry her. If it had been jarring, if he'd hated it, then their personalities would probably have clashed so that they wouldn't have set up housekeeping together at all. Or shouldn't have.

An associate of mine tells of setting up the first apartment she and her husband had. They had enough furniture from their two small apartments to fill the large one they took, and it blended well. Only one thing had to be settled. They had a single bed and a three-quarter bed and the question was whether to buy twins or a king-sized one. For the sake of comfort he opted for the twins. She said, "If we have separate beds we might as well have separate rooms. And if we have separate rooms we might as well live on separate continents."

*The raised fireplace in the bedroom as seen from our bed.*

They're now happily sleeping in a king-sized bed, his side firmly tucked in, and hers looking as if a hurricane had struck it.

That's my feeling about bedrooms too, and I feel that they should be very feminine. I know a rather famous couple whose bedroom is all in a man's colors—browns and beiges for the drapes, carpet and bedspread, and dark masculine mahogany furniture. But I think men feel much more masculine walking from a brown or green dressing room into a lovely feminine bedroom.

Of course if there is enough space each should have a dressing room. And a man could have a small bed in his for the times that he has to work late or get up very early and doesn't want to disturb his wife. Alfred and I each had our own commodious dressing rooms, and on the landing outside, before you entered my dressing room, was a little compartment for instant snacks. Behind a sliding door was a small icebox that held milk, cream, fruit, cheese, and splits of champagne. Above were shelves holding individual packages of cereal, and china, silver, and glassware.

Some views of the bedroom and dressing room. There was a fountain near the breakfast table.

Sometimes Alfred would be so terribly tired that he'd go to bed and sleep for an hour or two. When he woke, completely rested, he'd be ravenous. He'd have a snack and sit up and read for a while, and neither of us had to go downstairs.

That apartment had tall ceilings and I was able to have a double-decker dressing room, with my out-of-season clothes stored up top. Then twice a year I'd switch them around. Of course now that I travel so much—leaving here in a blizzard and arriving somewhere else the same night in 120 degrees of heat—I have to have everything at hand. A good thing, since my present ceilings aren't high enough for that double-decker arrangement. But if you can do it, it's a very practical device and a space-saver.

I think one of the most important things in decorating is that you should like every room in the house or apartment. If you find yourself always avoiding one of the rooms, something's wrong. Find out what. Maybe the furniture is all right, but the color of the walls or the curtains is wrong. Study it. Don't waste a room because you don't feel right in it. Every room should be designed for happy living. I think that was the secret of the success of our apartment.

Billy Haines likes to begin working with a client even before the architect is chosen, and he starts with the kitchen because he starts with living. How do you live? Do you love to eat well, entertain, sit with your family and friends around the kitchen table? That's the heart of the home. Everything else branches out from there. Then, of course, he wants to know your feelings about color. First for the drawing room, because that's the room that explains you to your friends, defines your personality. When they walk in there it tells them so much about you.

As for periods and styles, he maintains that people who have a natural interest in decorating start out from the worst, go through all possible periods, and then end up with that first period again—but this time with their taste so cultivated and improved that it works. You can't teach people taste. They're born with it—born with a desire for it, perhaps without knowing it.

We learn through exposure: seeing good homes, looking at good paintings, studying good window displays as we walk down the avenue, as we go to art galleries. Perhaps we can't afford all the things we see, but by observing we learn what we would like to live with. You see a color as you pass a shop. You may pass it three times. It's still there. It could be a wall, or a color in a painting. Then you go in and ask about it. It belongs to you by then. It has your name on it. And aren't we lucky when it's not too expensive! As I was exposed I learned. And as I learned I adopted a color, or an idea. Then I started to be a little bit courageous on my own.

People who have good taste are bound to make a mistake now and then, because they're human, and when they do it's a horrendous one. It's so ugly you can't believe it. On the other hand people who have terrible taste are bound to make a mistake and buy something exquisite—and you can't possibly understand how *that* could happen!

I'll admit that a lot of money had gone into my homes, because home life has always meant so very much to me. But money has nothing to do with taste. Money buys luxury, that's all. It buys a fabric hand woven to order—but not necessarily a beautiful one. Today, with all the wonderful decorating magazines and the reams of advice that pour off the presses every week, there is no reason for people having homes that aren't warm, attractive, and inviting.

One way to find out the kind of rooms you'll be happy in is to buy the good decorating magazines and tear out pictures that catch your eye, that make you say, "How lovely!" If you spread them out on a big table you'll probably find that they all have something in common. Certain colors or color combinations will probably predominate. And a certain ambiance—maybe you'll find yourself attracted to sparsely furnished rooms with an Oriental flavor, polished surfaces, clean lines. Or maybe it will be heavy, traditional, or Provincial, with a safe, in-out-of-the-cold feeling. Then see whether your husband is attracted to the same pictures.

With taste, and a little study and ingenuity, any woman can have a perfectly lovely place. Lacking taste? Ask! Any good store will happily give you expert advice. If you can't afford that, look —feel—observe. And your friends will be enchanted to tell you what to do. (Be sure they're friends with beautiful homes.)

But before she takes even expert advice, a woman should know a lot about herself before she starts putting money into furniture. It's a question of age, too. A young bride probably has a lot of growing and developing to do. I know I did, and that's why I tried so many styles before I found my own.

There come periods in your life when you'll have to do a lot of discarding. Usually it's when you're moving. They tell me that an average American family moves every four years. That must be quite a trauma. I really feel for those families who have to uproot themselves because the men are promoted and transferred. But that seems to be the American way of business.

I've heard of men who were permanently stymied in their careers because their wives flatly refused to leave their home towns. That's not right. A man's job has to come first and women have to draw on their natural adaptability. Moving from Cleveland to Pittsburgh, after all, isn't like moving from Paris to Tokyo. The language is the same, there are the same chain stores and supermarkets—and the same kind of people. Being a joiner helps. Women who naturally gravitate to the church, the women's club, the Red Cross, or whatever, will feel as if they've never left home.

The same brand of coffee and conversation is served up. The skirts are the same length, and the domestic problems are the same. Young children, especially if they're shy, may have a few problems at first, but no adult woman should flip over having to put down new roots.

I read a lovely story once about a woman who did a lot of moving around. Everywhere she went she planted a tree. A little bit of herself was left behind for the next occupant to enjoy, and occasionally she was able to revisit one of "her" trees to see how it had grown. She was never rootless! She must have been a very nice person.

Moving is hard work for a couple of weeks, but it pays off in broader horizons and a cluster of new friends. I don't think a woman ever needs to feel alone in this world as long as she can put on a hat and go out and say "Hello! How are you?" Be flexible. Back up your husband and give him the support he needs. That move might be more of a strain for him than it is for you. A new boss is more of a problem than the length of your curtains or the chore of finding a new dentist for the children.

After we were married in 1955 I kept the house in Los Angeles for a while. But we spent so little time there that I finally put it on the market. When it was sold I had just five days to pack. I had lived there since 1929—twenty-six years—and it was crammed with things I loved. But I had to give up most of them because there was no room in New York, even in that large apartment. Lovely Georgian silver . . . well-loved books . . . I had to be ruthless. I tore through the place like a whirlwind.

"This is to be auctioned. These to be given to my daughters. This to be given to charity. That to pack for New York."

I kept the books I couldn't bear to part with—classics, and autographed volumes by old friends—and gave the rest to Brandeis University, together with my awards—except for my Oscar, my Cecil B. de Mille award and my "Pally" award. There's a Joan Crawford School of Dance at Brandeis where they'll have a good home.

If I'd had two months to make that move I'd have sent everything on, paid the freight, and then had to get rid of it after all. So I'm glad it was a quick, clean break. It's the best way to do it. I've never regretted a single thing left there. It's gone; forget it. I found I had to be ruthless about possessions or they would possess me.

My next move was from the big Fifth Avenue duplex to the much smaller apartment I live in now. That wasn't quite such a

*My present apartment has a long, wide entrance hall. The dining room is on the right.*

wrenching experience. For one thing, I only had a few blocks to go. But I had to dispose of a great many things and again it was a question of deciding what to send to Parke-Bernet for auctioning because I have much less storage space here for china and crystal.

Before a thing was packed we measured each wall in the new apartment and then went back and measured every piece of furniture—chairs, couches, tables, everything. When the right place was found for each piece it was labeled—"living room, west wall," "dining room," "master bedroom," and so on. Moving day was relatively painless. The real secret was careful planning. All the work was done weeks before at my desk, and when M-Day came it all went off like a breeze. All the packing of breakables was entrusted to the moving men because they're experts (and beside, they're insured). I find that moving men respond nicely to a bright smile, too, and the offer of coffee or a soft drink in the middle of a hard morning's work. In that move, not a thing was broken or damaged, and everything was set down in the right place.

I have the lovely upholstered pieces that were made for the Fifth Avenue apartment, and some of the fine Chinese pieces I acquired in California. My living- and dining-room walls, and those in the hall, are white. The sofas are egg-yolk yellow—not a metallic gold shade, which I find harsh. The linen draperies, too, which I brought from the other apartment and had shortened, are egg-yolk yellow with white linen behind them. (When they're washed only one set is taken down at a time, so that there's always something at the windows.)

The yellow is a lovely soft background for the leaf-green accents on small chairs and stools. The sofas are banked with green and yellow pillows, sparked with two chintz pillows in green and white. The same colors flow into the dining room, which seats eight very comfortably and ten if necessary, at a yellow baked-enamel Parsons table that I have covered with yellow felt for everyday wear and tear. The dining-room curtains have a pale-green-and-white floral design. The chairs are covered in green leather.

The living room is L-shaped, giving the effect of two rooms, and in each I have a large green area rug bordered in yellow. Lamps, sculpture, and bibelots, some I've had for decades, stand out strikingly against the white walls. And there are masses of green plants and flowers at all times of the year. There's a long

*In the living room are some of the art objects we bought on our travels.*

low breakfront displaying the miniatures I've always loved collecting, and the hall is lined, floor to ceiling, with bookshelves
containing books I've managed to keep with me from other years,
and the new ones that seem to come in every day.

I've said that I avoid chintz, but very bravely I've added an armchair done in the same pattern as the pillows and the dining-room curtains and it's a great improvement. It softens and warms the room.

One of the reasons I hesitate about chintz is my paintings. A good collection of oils is busy enough for one room or one area. It takes time to decide where they should go, too. All the furniture should be in place first. Each house or apartment is different, so paintings are the last things I arrange, and I do it with great love and care. There's a little anecdote about my collection.

A couple of weeks after Alfred's funeral Jerry Wald phoned me and said, "I've got a part for you. It's a small one, it's a cameo, but I think work is the best therapy for you."

It was *The Best of Everything*, to be directed by Jean Negulesco. Jean had directed me in *Humoresque* and so, without hesitating, I said, "I'll take it."

"Don't you want to read the script?"

"No," I said, "I trust you. Thank you for thinking of me."

Jean collected a great many Dufys, Buffets, and others when they could be bought cheaply, and had a fine collection. One day on the set, in front of the entire cast, he said, "Joan Crawford has the most spectacular penthouse in New York City, but the lousiest taste in paintings."

I said, "You know, Jean, my husband and I picked up our paintings along the way because each one held a certain memory for us that meant so much to our married life. So to each his own, but don't criticize other people. I have to live with those paintings, and by God I'm very happy living with them!"

I almost cried. It was only a few weeks since Alfred had been buried. But I was so mad at Jean it kept me from crying. Now, every time I look at the Jamaican things I remember Negulesco. But I have so many other lovely memories, too, of the places we

74

went, the things we did. We didn't buy willy-nilly. I remember how we happened across one of the paintings in a little studio behind a barber shop. The barber, Herbert Palmer, was a fine primitive painter and dashed back there to work between customers. It was love at first sight because it expressed everything we felt about Jamaica and the colors were strong and beautiful. You have to live with a painting as you do with a lover. It's that personal. You might want to change lovers. You might want to rearrange your paintings. That's the way it should be.

I'm beginning to run out of wall space. I have Margaret Keane's paintings, which I love, hanging in my bedroom and dressing room, and I think I would start putting them in the bathrooms if the walls weren't tiled to the ceilings.

I keep a very tiny pad in Beverly Hills because I'm in and out of there quite often, and it also serves as an office for Betty Barker. The first floor is done in Chinese modern with a great big Chinese coffee table and a huge coral sofa with green cushions. The dining room is really just an alcove with a curved wall. There's a lovely circular staircase and two bedrooms upstairs, and a tiny garden in back. It's like a doll's house, and a very cozy place to stay on my short visits to the Coast, instead of a hotel.

I think there's still another move in my future. I'm going to build a small house in the country, I don't know where. But away from the city. Away from the soot and smog, the sirens and the pressures.

# ·IV·

## The Pleasure of Company

A LOVELY HOME means two things to me. First of all it's a cocoon in which to wrap a happy marriage. And second, it's a place to welcome friends, make them comfortable and give them delicious things to eat. If I hadn't become an actress I'm sure I'd have made a good chef, or a restaurateur. Cooking to please other people is one of the things I love best.

When Helen Hayes and Bethel Leslie came to stay with me in California, I had a really challenging hostess task. They were there for ten days. During the day there were story conferences at Paramount. But each night, for ten nights, I had a dinner party for eighteen. Helen, of course, wanted to see all her friends and I thought that if they all swarmed in at once for a big cocktail party or buffet she'd hardly get a chance to say more than hello to any one of them.

So there were just eighteen every night because that was the number that could be seated in my dining room. Before, during, and after dinner she had a chance for a good chat with everyone. My cook—what a gem she was—never had a day off, but she had help. I had double service, so there were two butlers and four maids, all doing their jobs efficiently and quietly. While we had our first course, two of the maids would tidy up the drawing room, cleaning the ashtrays and clearing away the hors d'oeuvres and glasses. Then they were ready to help the butlers serve extra things like bread and butter. The other two helped clear away between courses and cleaned up. The butler's pantry was so separated from the dining room that we couldn't hear the clatter they must have been making.

I had to create ten different menus, but that wasn't a problem. Good food is one of my passions and it's easy for me to dream up dinner menus. I varied the table settings, too. I've always collected lovely cloths and serviettes, and I have extra-large place mats made to order. I like mats big enough to hold the whole service including the salad and the wine glass neatly. I've collected fabrics for my table from as far away as Beirut.

Needless to say, the porcelain and crystal sparkled, the silver was polished until it reflected, and the table was lit by candles and soft wall sconces. Flower arrangements were low so that people didn't have to crane their necks to see who was on the other side of the table.

Billy Haines gave me an important rule for entertaining. We were giving a party and I said, "Billy, I don't think I can handle two hundred people. I think I'll have them here for cocktails and then take them to Chasen's, where I'll have a private room prepared for us."

He said, "Never move your party—except from one area to another in your own home." I often entertain in restaurants these days, and I reserve two rooms. One for cocktails, the other for the dinner. But the *party* isn't moved.

I had a large patio back of my living room and library. There was an expanse of lawn sloping downward with about ten steps in the middle. The sides were planted with geraniums, zinnias, and other flowers in all the brilliant colors I could find. For that party and many others I had cocktails on the patio and on the lower part of the lawn with tables that seated six.

Beyond was the swimming pool, where I floated gardenias and

candles. On one side was the bathhouse, on the other, the theater. The badminton court and the pergola were at the back of the property. We put a dance floor on the badminton court and had two services, one at each end, so there wouldn't be a bottleneck at either table. There were beautiful hot things—suckling pig, roast beef, crisp roast legs of lamb, golden squabs. And trays of fresh green vegetables, and lots of cold salads. Tables for ten were placed under the pergola, with place cards for two hundred. Even with a buffet, people *must* sit down to eat. You just can't ask guests to stand around balancing a plate, silver, a serviette, and trying to find a fourth hand for a glass of wine.

On evenings like that it was like fairyland, with the candles reflected in the pool and the soft indirect lighting on the trees and shrubbery. I loved it as much as my guests did.

Noel Coward once said, "Joan not only *gives* a party, she *goes* to it!"

I think that's one secret of a good party: all the arrangements

*Entertaining at home means planning and preparation . . . and then the hostess can enjoy herself.*

seem as effortless as if they floated down from a nearby cloud and the hostess has nothing to do but enjoy herself. Those were the most extravagant days of my life.

Another important party secret is knowing how to mix people. Or, simply, knowing that you *should* mix them. Ev and Harold Glasser know this, and I always find a fascinating collection of people at their famous dinner parties. They have, to begin with, one of the most perfect settings I've ever seen, with wall-to-wall windows overlooking all of Manhattan, halfway up in the sky. They've decorated with clean lines, warm colors, and some priceless Chinese furniture—an orange lacquer screen, and an enormous Chinese red lacquer coffee table that blends with good traditional things. They bring in plenty of help. Three in the kitchen, two maids, and a butler handle twenty people for a sit-down dinner. Everything is stage-managed to perfection. But it's the people they invite who really make a good evening.

How often have you heard people say, "Oh, I can't ask the Smiths to the same party with the Kellys. They have nothing in common."

How do you know? How do you know, in fact, that their having nothing in common isn't the very thing that will make them interesting to each other? David Frost recently asked Paul Newman what he and Joanne Woodward had in common. "Absolutely nothing," Paul said, "but she's a great broad!" There's nothing duller than a gathering of people who are in the same business, or who have the same hobby, or the same education, or are the same age. What do they have to ask each other? What do they have to learn?

The best parties are a wild mixture. Take some corporation presidents, add a few lovely young actresses, a bearded painter, a professional jockey, your visiting friends from Brussels, a politician, a hairdresser, and a professor of physics, toss them all together, and try to get them to stop talking long enough to eat! It's especially important to have all age groups. I've never noticed any generation gap. Of course I wouldn't want to have hippies come crawling in with unwashed feet, but all the younger people I know are bright and attractive and have something to say. They also dress like human beings. They love to listen, too. They make wonderful guests.

After that kind of party people will say, "I had the most wonderful evening. Let me tell you who I met . . . or what Doctor So-and-So said about . . ." And they'll look forward to the next one.

If you go along with the "common interest" theory you'll have prospective guests saying to each other, "Oh, not that again! They'll have Stuart and Jane, and Ken and Jean, and Ben and

Alice, all saying the same things that we've been hearing for years." It's much more fun if they know they're going to get some surprises.

Some people tend to serve the same food each time they entertain, too. Probably because it's foolproof. And so guests come knowing they're going to get sliced ham, or a Stroganoff, or whatever your specialty is. Practice new ideas when it's just the family, and provide some surprises in the culinary department. Just about the only time *not* to try anything new is when the boss is coming for dinner. That's usually a prospect that makes any young bride want to crawl into the closet and lock the door.

There are rules about that kind of little dinner party. Wear a simple dress in which you always feel comfortable, prepare a simple meal that's always a success. Forget the Iranian caviar and the beef Wellington. After all, the boss knows what your husband's salary is, and if you spend a week's salary trying to impress him, you *will*—you'll impress him as being foolish and extravagant. You may hire a maid to help with serving and clearing away, but don't pretend she's permanent help. It's a silly kind of lie. Don't talk too much, and above all, don't drink too much. That's the evening to sip a little vermouth or white wine before dinner, even if the boss and his wife have three martinis.

A superb hostess who's been giving great parties for years plays a role she knows by heart. But a nervous or inexperienced one can benefit by some rehearsing. I don't mean rehearsing the salad dressing, but rehearsing *herself*. I know a charming woman who was always tongue-tied at her own parties although she was perfectly at ease in other people's houses. So a hundred times she practiced walking around her living room chatting with imaginary guests. Finding the right thing to say to each one. Introducing strangers with just the right phrase to interest them in one another. She practiced moving gracefully, going to the door to greet newcomers, offering canapés. And now she thoroughly enjoys going to her *own* parties.

There's nothing silly about rehearsing. Red Skelton, I am told, practiced a routine thousands of times in his bedroom before he dared try it on a stage, and Billy Graham, they tell me, preached sermons to trees before he faced an audience.

Rehearse your dress, too. Whether you're having only six for dinner or fifty for cocktails, wear a lovely gown. A hostess has earned the right to look special. When all the other ladies wear short skirts, she can look smashing in a long one, or in hostess pajamas. She can sparkle, glitter, and greet her guests in a riot of color. It's her special privilege.

And these days, when men are blossoming out with more color and originality, I think the host can wear something more daring than a dark-blue business suit. I don't mean that he should look like a clown—and I've met a few men at dinner parties who looked as if they were trying out for Barnum and Bailey's new season. But he might wear a velvet smoking jacket, or a bright silk ascot. After all, he is at home—and if he looks attractive and relaxed, his guests will be too.

It doesn't necessarily take money (though that helps) to have successful parties, large or small. It's possible to give a lovely buffet dinner for twelve people—my favorite number—with just one reliable person to help. The secret is in the planning. If you've done your advance work and you're well organized, no one will guess that you haven't a backstairs staff of six, and you'll have the feeling that when your guests have left all the dishes will be done and the dining room set in order again. That's when it's like "going to your own party."

If you can spare a few extra dollars, there should be a bar-

*When it's a surprise party it has to be at a restaurant. This was Alfred's birthday party at "21" in 1957. Mrs. Alfred Bloomingdale and I watched him blow out the candles.*

tender for the first part of your party. No man can enjoy himself if he's glued to the bar mixing drinks for a dozen people, and getting them all mixed up when he tries to talk to a guest. Sometimes a close man friend will agree to take over the job, but a paid bartender, perhaps a college boy, is a good investment in relaxation. Then he can police the living room, gathering up glasses and emptying ashtrays, while your guests are serving themselves in the dining room.

I'm always acutely uncomfortable if I see my hostess rushing off to the kitchen or fretting so about her arrangements that she hasn't even time to chat with her guests. The art of gracious living is fast disappearing. Overelaborate parties aren't in good taste. But a relaxed and happy hostess is one of the few things we have left from a more leisurely era. Planning and organizing can make you one of those fortunate ladies.

Having decided on the mixture and number of guests, and the stunning gown you'll wear, you can get down to the delicious job of deciding what to serve and how to serve it.

I have some strict rules about how food is presented. Hot food must be on hot plates. It's no problem to put the plates in the oven after the roast has been turned down, and I think it's an insult to a guest to offer meat on a plate that's come right out of the cupboard.

Salads must be served on cold plates, and so must cold desserts. There's nothing easier than to stack them in the refrigerator for a couple of hours. Butter should come on a bed of crushed ice, and hot bread should be kept hot in a napkin or a bread warmer. No drips—when meat is put onto a serving platter there's bound to be a little splatter, but it should be wiped clean before it's brought into the dining room.

When I plan a menu I consider color, texture, taste, and balance:

*Color:* A red vegetable next to a yellow one looks unappetizing. Two white ones, like celery and cauliflower, look awful.

*Texture:* Creamed chicken with mashed potatoes makes too much mush. Always serve something crisp with something soft.

*Taste:* Never team two sours, two sweets, or two bitters. Candied yams and cranberry sauce are both delectable, but served together they break two of these rules, color and taste contrast.

*Balance:* Courses shouldn't be uniformly rich nor light. A too-rich menu might consist of a heavy cream soup, a roast with thickened gravy and potatoes, and a heavy whipped-cream-topped dessert. If the main course is substantial the first should be light, crisp, and appetizing and the dessert an airy sherbet or a compote of fresh fruit.

I decide first on the main course. For a buffet for twelve there should be two warm dishes. If you're going to be a relaxed hostess choose two that can be made the day before. Most of them improve with reheating. Some of the possibilities are beef bourguignon, boned and skinned breasts of chicken in a delicate cream sauce, a shrimp-lobster-and-scallop Newburg, lamb curry with all its interesting accompaniments.

With any of these, serve a large, icy bowl of crisp salad with a choice of two or three dressings in little bowls alongside.

Hot dishes must be kept hot in chafing dishes or on a hot tray so that they're just as good for the second helping. Plates should be brought warm to the buffet table just before the guests serve themselves. I like to have a complete service at each end of the table so that people won't have to stand in line forever, and there should be an attractive centerpiece, though it can be very simple. A bowl of flowers, carefully arranged by the hostess in the afternoon, and candles—always candlelight.

The first course for a buffet supper should be an eye-catching array of canapés served in the living room with the drinks. I think there should be one interesting hot thing, one at room temperature, and a bouquet of crisp raw vegetables.

The raw vegetables might include slim carrot sticks, green pepper slices, scallions, little love tomatoes, zucchini wedges, radishes, cauliflowerettes, olives, and young turnips. Arrange them colorfully in a large bowl over crushed ice and offer a couple of dips for non-dieters.

Here are some of the hot hors d'oeuvres that I love (and they must be *kept* hot in chafing dishes):

I sauté half-strips of bacon in butter until it's *half* done and wrap the strips around chicken livers or pimiento-stuffed olives. They go into a preheated oven (350 degrees) and bake until the bacon is crisp.

I use a little round cookie cutter to make rounds of very thin white bread, then I toast them in the oven, buttered, spread them with peanut butter, and stick them under the broiler until they're piping hot. I sprinkle crisp, crumbled bacon all over the top.

Ev Glasser presented us with an absolute delight one evening. She drops spoonfuls of potato-pancake batter into deep fat for just a few seconds and serves them with sour cream and Iranian caviar. The combination of flavors is angelic.

Some other combinations I like:

Paper-thin slices of prosciutto wrapped around a slice of melon or a slice of fresh fig or a wedge of fresh pear.

Rolled smoked salmon on thinly sliced pumpernickel with capers and lemon wedges.

And an accidental discovery of mine. I had two kinds of salami on hand one day, one moist and one dry. I made a little sandwich with a moist slice, then a little mustard, then the dry slice, and a cocktail onion on top, all held together with a toothpick.

Cheese puffs are always popular, but they're an awful bore unless they're made with very sharp cheddar and a touch of hot mustard, and really puffed up. And *hot*.

Meat balls are a faithful favorite. They should be very highly seasoned, served with a mustard or tomato sauce that has bite, and kept warm on a hotplate. It's best to serve hot hors d'oeuvres in two batches, the second ones heating under the broiler while the first round of drinks is served.

# The Pleasure of Company

After your helper has dealt with the canapés she can put the finishing touches on the buffet table, and I hope that your supper is being run on a strict schedule.

I have strong feelings about people who issue invitations to come at seven and don't open the dining-room doors until nine-thirty. So I always ask, "And what time is *dinner? Nine?*" Fine. I get there a little after eight. An hour is long enough to drink. After two and a half hours people are sodden and not very amusing—and furthermore they can't appreciate or even taste the food the hostess has gone to such trouble to prepare. And the nondrinkers are starved and bored. With this system I gain more time at my desk, too. Precious time.

By the same token, there's no excuse for people who arrive late. The hostess has planned her dinner and the cook has it in perfect condition at the announced time. Fifteen minutes' delay—let alone half an hour—may ruin it. A distinguished elderly couple who get about quite a bit in New York are forthright about this kind of thing when they're guests. If the hostess holds dinner for a late arrival the gentleman will look at his watch and say, "Dinner is ten minutes late. If Ernesta doesn't have her bale of hay on time she gets very bad tempered!"

George Washington, a gregarious man who always had guests at every meal, would say to latecomers, "Gentlemen, I have a cook who never asks whether the company has come, but whether the hour has come."

We should all be brave enough to say that. A carefully planned dinner should never be ruined by rudeness.

While your guests are serving themselves in the dining room your helper should dash into the living room to collect all the debris—the leftover canapés, the glasses and dirty ashtrays—

87

plump up the pillows, and put clean ashtrays around. Then people can come back to an uncluttered place. Little individual tables are a good idea and should be set up at the same time.

After people have had their second helpings the maid clears the buffet and puts out the dessert. Some people like an elaborate ice-cream concoction—so many men like gooey, sweet things. Pander to them, and let *them* worry about their waistlines. Some people like to end a dinner with cheese and fruit. Offer two kinds—one bland and one forthright, and just ripe. French bread and crackers on the side. For diet watchers have a pretty bowl of fresh fruits, dewy and very cold. Serve good, strong coffee in pretty demitasses and let the relaxed conversation take over.

Sunday brunch is an easy, pleasant way to entertain a largish group, especially in the country. Americans who overslept invented the word brunch, but the ingredients and the casual atmosphere bear a strong resemblance to breakfast in an English country house or to a French midnight supper. The choice of menu can be as wide as the imagination. Practically anything goes—from hearty breakfast dishes such as filled omelettes, kidneys, chicken livers and bacon, sausages, and to eggs Benedict. Something pretty in aspic, or a salmon mousse in a fish-shaped mold, makes a lovely centerpiece. Best of all, most of the meal can be prepared way ahead of time and it can be managed without any outside help—if, that is, the hostess puts in a lot of work the day before and early that morning.

People can wander in when they feel like it, so there's no need to time this one. Drinks are no problem. A big punch bowl with chunks of fresh fruit makes a nice starter, and the mixings for bloody Marys, screwdrivers, or bullshots can be left on a table for guests to serve themselves. Of course there should be a big pot of very good coffee.

Being a guest involves some responsibility, too. I always go up and introduce myself to strangers. After all, the host and hostess can't be everywhere at once.

I say, "Hello! I'm Joan Crawford."

Usually they'll laugh and say, "You have to be kidding. We'd never know it."

So in my case it may be funny. But you can't just stand around and wait for introductions and entertainment. Say, "I'm Anita Johnson. We moved here recently from Chicago." And off you go. The other person's sure to know somebody in Chicago, and your hostess will be relieved. Another of my tricks is to go to the end of the room where there are fewer people. Most parties seem to bottleneck at one end. A guest can be a great help in getting the crowd circulating more freely.

I do very little large-scale entertaining in my present apartment. The main reason is that I'm at my desk all day, and having even a few people for dinner means that I'd want to be in the kitchen instead. There's just no time. Occasionally I have a catered sit-down dinner for ten. It's the right number for my dining room, and the right number for conversation.

On the other hand, I love cooking a "family" dinner for just two or three old friends, or my daughters. There's no formality then. I do simple things like pork chops with purple onions and fried apple rings, boiled beef or chicken, or meat loaf.

I use two pounds of ground sirloin, a pound of ground veal, and a pound of sausage meat for the meat loaf, thoroughly mixed with three eggs, a bottle of A-1, a good lacing of Worcestershire, a lot of seasoned salt, and finely chopped purple onion and green peppers. I hide four hard-boiled eggs inside the loaf and before it goes into the oven I dribble over more A-1 and Worcestershire and seasoned salt so that a crust will form. Sliced hot or cold, this is a combination I can vouch for.

One of my favorite salads is wilted spinach. I pour hot bacon grease and vinegar over the spinach leaves until they sag, and then sprinkle crisp bacon on top. You can do this with lettuce or dandelion greens, too.

Another good salad I sometimes serve with fried chicken or baked ham is made with kidney beans, purple onions, green peppers, celery, and hot red peppers—all chopped very fine and tossed with vinegar, Tabasco, kosher salt, and black pepper. It should be refrigerated overnight to marinate, so that all the flavors blend together.

I must brag, finally, that I'm famous, among a small group of regulars, for my coleslaw. The basic ingredients are shaved cabbage, green peppers, finely chopped pimiento, and pineapple.

*Ivan Rebroff, the great Russian baritone, called when he was in New York for a concert. He was curious to see what an Oscar looked and felt like. It's heavy!*

*I love having in one dear friend, like Anita Loos, very informally. The menu is pork chops and fried apple rings, and two places are laid at the game table in the living room.*

Over this goes a dressing of mayonnaise, a liberal amount of both dry mustard and prepared mustard, the juice of six lemons, olive oil, cider vinegar, hot peppers, and a magic mixture of spices and herbs that I buy from a restaurant in Hollywood, the Cock 'n Bull.

Food! I say "No, thank you" to many lovely things every day. Recently I admired the slim figure of a magazine editor. "What's your formula?" I asked her.

"I starve," she sighed. "I'm the hungriest woman in New York."

Our director of public relations, Bob Kelly, told me that someone is working on a pill that will adjust the metabolism so that we can eat anything we want. I think he was only kidding— but if not, I hope they hurry up and perfect it. Good food is one of life's great joys.

I gave a party for Sir Noel Coward at "21" shortly after he was knighted. Above, Mitchell Cox, Noel holding Lynn Fontanne's hand, and Mainbocher at right. Below, left to right, Radie Harris of the Hollywood Reporter, Mitchell Cox, myself and Noel.

## The Pleasure of Company

I have two golden rules for houseguesting:

1. I wouldn't have—or be—a houseguest if I didn't know the people very well.

2. I stay out of their hair.

A houseguest can disrupt an entire household. When I stayed with Lynn and Alfred Lunt on their lovely farm in Wisconsin they told me that their custom—a very nice one for a guest—was to give the breakfast order the night before, and then ring when it was wanted. There was never a sound until I pressed the button that told the kitchen, "I'm up. You can prepare it now." They would never let a houseguest go down for breakfast.

Then I'd appear whenever I felt like it. If I had a script to prepare I just stayed in my room. I knew what time lunch was, and I showed up then. If there was reading I wanted to do I pretended I was sleeping in. Of course, sleeping in, to me, means nine-thirty. I've always been a very early riser.

When Gwen Verdon visited the Lunts she had just finished a show and she was absolutely bushed. She had a little nap, joined them for dinner, and then went back to bed at nine. The next day at one-fifteen they waked her and said, "We're sorry, dear, but you have a plane to make." How she had slept in that wonderful air and comfort!

At Lynn and Alfred's, each room has a different character. The drawing room is formal. Then there are smaller rooms for tea or cocktails, and three more rooms to pass through before you reach the dining room. Each one has a different mood—they are really like a succession of stage settings—but all are light and airy and filled with the things the Lunts have collected through the years. The kitchen is an important part of the house because divine food is part of their lives. Alfred is a master chef and has taught Jules, once his dresser in the theater, all the tricks of the culinary art.

Outside are magnificent gardens. The late, lamented duck, Walter, made them his domain. He would waddle happily along behind Lynn as she wandered around with her little basket gathering things, but he hated Alfred.

"Joan, I don't know why, but he just loathes me," Alfred would say. "He came up behind me once, very sneakily. I was bending over, pruning my roses. And he bit me right on my ass! He really bites. He went through my trousers!"

"But didn't you turn the other cheek, dear?" I asked him sweetly.

There are some murals in the Lunts' house, some done by a prominent artist and one rather special one done by Alfred. He took me into their guest house to show it to me. There was Adam on one side, and Eve on the other. I frowned, puzzled. Alfred watched me with a little smile. Finally he said, "I know, they're odd—you see, Lynn posed for both of them."


When I stay with friends in the country I like to take long walks, especially if it's spring or fall. I know poison ivy and poison oak when I see them and I give them a wide berth. If there are no servants I offer to help in the kitchen, but if they say no, I stay out. That means the kitchen's too small for three or four of us, and I respect that. I wouldn't want too many people in mine—unless it's the big country kitchen I'm planning next.

What I really prefer, though, is to keep out of people's hair by staying at a nearby hotel. I can take my long walks without thinking, My God, I have to be back for lunch in ten minutes—how far away am I? I enjoy the quiet days outdoors by myself, and I go to my host and hostess for dinner. So I'm not a problem and everybody's more relaxed.

As for gifts, if I haven't seen the house before, I wait until afterward so that I can choose something that will fit in. But I often send flowers in advance. Not big tall things that have to stand in a corner, but low round bowls that can be seen from every side and that can be placed on an odd table somewhere.

Having houseguests I think really requires as much help as you can possibly afford. If you plan dinner parties you have to have someone to serve and clean up. A *minimum* of one. I'd rather save pennies and have guests only once a year, with enough staff to run everything beautifully, than to have to spend all my time in the kitchen, knowing that the ashtrays weren't being emptied and the dirty dishes had to be dealt with surreptitiously in the middle of the night. Having houseguests should be fun, not drudgery.

Their time shouldn't be organized, either. You can smother them to death with plans for every minute. Maybe they want to sleep all morning. Maybe they *don't* want to see the local scenic wonders or watch little Johnny in the school play. Let them amuse themselves as they like during the day and just see them every night for dinner. Find out if they want to meet people. If they do, organize cocktail or dinner parties. If they don't, tip off the friendly neighbors that your guests are very eccentric or suffering from a contagious disease.

Above all be sure that you're very fond of the people you ask to come and stay. Some beautiful friendships have been ship-wrecked over a long weekend.

# ·V·

## Over the Garden Gate

I've worked all my life. True, I didn't get my first professional dancing job until the advanced age of fourteen, but I'd done many a long day's work before that, helping my mother and trying to get myself through school. I can't imagine any other way of life.

But these days a lot of women are coming fresh into the business world who were brought up to believe that their only function in life was to please a man, run a home, and raise children. They go to work for a variety of reasons, and in such numbers that a working woman is the rule these days, rather than the exception.

One reason is money. People want more things. Once we demanded two chickens in every pot, then two cars in every garage. Now families want two homes—one a retreat for weekends and vacations—and maybe a boat or an airplane. So it follows that they need two pay checks.

Also, it costs a small fortune to send children through college these days—up to $15,000 or $20,000 per child. *Plus* those big wardrobes, all the changes of dresses that the girls want, the matching shoes that they *have* to have. Mother and daddy need about eighteen pay checks coming in, so there's no better incentive than that for mother to get out and scramble for the second one.

But all the working women I know—and I think that 98

percent of my women friends have jobs or professions—love their work because it adds so many extra dimensions to their lives. Because it gives them an identity, just as their husbands have. This is the most important reason of all for working. A home-bound woman who depends on bridge clubs and shopping sprees for amusement has only half a personality.

Usually she starts to realize this when her children are in school and have so many interests of their own that they barely manage to get home in time for dinner. Her husband's reaching the peak of his career and engrossed in it—sometimes to the point where he takes his briefcase into his study every night. Everybody seems to be involved in something *outside*. Everybody is taking mother for granted. They don't bother discussing things with her very much because her interests all *seem* to revolve around house-keeping and gossip, and her husband certainly doesn't want to hear how she killed the day at the country club. (If she can afford a club. I've given up my memberships. They're too expensive.)

The kids take mother for granted. They think that parents stop growing. They don't give them credit for keeping up with what's going on and so they just tune the "old folks" out. Those old folks in their late thirties!

This is crisis time. I call it the late-thirties syndrome. A smart woman asks herself questions: Who am I? What good am I any more? Who needs me? What have I got to talk about? And she takes some action.

But men, as I've noted before, are funny. They may be bored with their wives—but the idea of wives working, of having interesting careers of their own, sends some men straight up the wall. I think that if a woman decides to work her husband should have tremendous respect for her. I'd think his admiration should shoot sky-high—he ought to be deliciously happy.

But no, men put up all kinds of objections, all of which cover up their real, subconscious fear that "she'll come home tired and won't want to go to bed with me." They wonder what's going to happen to them sexually. But the fact is that when a woman feels she's done a good job and accomplished something, she's charged. She's ready for sex. Maybe *he'll* be too tired that night. And maybe he'll get raped!

When she goes back to work there'll be plenty of changes. If she used to wonder about the attractive women he was meeting during the day, now he can wonder about the attractive men *she's* working with. *She's* having those business luncheons, those stimulating discussions, contributing ideas of her own. She'll become a fascinating woman because she'll be an *interested* woman. Involved. Alive. He'll have to start worrying about whether *he* is being a bore!

Working couples have problems, and the wife has to solve most of them. She's got to face the fact that she's got at least three full-time jobs to cope with, and she's got to do them brilliantly. Whenever she slips up, her husband will say, "See? I told you it wouldn't work. Woman's place is in the home!"

But when she succeeds—and most women do—he's the proudest man alive. Proud that she's successful and confident and admired for her work; smugly pleased that she finds time to cater to his whims, take care of the children's needs, and keep the household running smoothly. Of course he wants to be smothered with affection and never feel that he's playing second string to a desk. But she loves him, so that part comes naturally.

I had a long talk recently with a couple who have both worked since the beginning of their marriage. They have two teenage children. She's a successful dress designer. He's a corporation lawyer. He didn't have the sudden shock of hearing, after fifteen years, that she had decided to go off to the marketplace and do her own thing because she was launched on her career before they decided to marry. But he's frank about the reservations he had at the time, and those that he still has to some extent. I think he has a typical male point of view.

"When I was first married," he told me, "I felt that no wife of mine should have to work, that I should be the sole support and carry all the burdens. And too, part of what a man bargains for in marriage is that he's getting someone who'll assume all the household responsibilities. This is extremely important."

Well Bill, as I'll call him, very tersely expressed all the traditional, centuries-old feelings of the protective male—and the dominating one. There's a slight edge of threat—but who's being threatened? The caveman went off for weeks at a time to find the meat to slaughter, leaving the cavewoman alone in the cave with the children, keeping the fire going, growing the grain and grinding it, and fending off all the local dangers. This was a real division of labor. He wasn't leaving her to the tender luxuries of a maid and a television set, a supermarket and a police force. And it occurs to me that some of those cavewomen might have preferred going off to slaughter the meat. Maybe they didn't like the job of keeping the cave going and raising the young all alone.

So the fact is women have always done a full-time job. They just didn't get paid for it. Until recently they *couldn't* get paid for it. Men had decided that their wives' only capabilities lay in the bedroom, the kitchen and the nursery even though a few lucky females have had the luck or the perseverance to rate a place in history—Cleopatra, Catherine the Great, George Sand, Marie Curie and Florence Nightingale, to name only a handful.

By now, women have proved that they can excel in every single branch of human endeavor (including carrying a gun, as Russian and Israeli women do). And most men will concede that they have the brains and often the brawn to do it. But most husbands want to make exceptions of their own wives.

Bill said, "A couple has to decide that this is the most compatible way for them to live. But a career has got to be very important to the woman. It must give her fulfillment. It has to be in her genes to have to work."

Maybe he thought they had to be odd genes—not quite feminine ones? His wife, Caroline, is the most feminine of women—and he knows it. Then we discussed some of the real questions that arise with a two-income marriage. They are mostly economic ones.

"Particularly in his younger years," Bill said, "a man finds himself adjusting to the higher income. He gets accustomed to it. He likes it. It becomes increasingly difficult to think of reducing his standard of living. It gives them a larger house or apartment and extra vacations. She's able to earn a fur coat and pay for a maid she might have had to wait ten years for him to provide as the sole wage earner. It can be dangerous.

"When the couple have everything they need, they begin to buy luxuries they don't need. They get careless. They pay higher prices because she has less time to shop. She pays someone else to do things a wife would normally do herself."

Now I don't like that view at all. If a woman can earn money to buy lovely things while she's young, she should have the privilege. I know a woman who said once, "I've worked all my life. And now that I can afford to buy myself diamonds, my hands are too old."

This woman was only forty-eight or fifty but she had work hands, ugly hands, that were no fit background for the beautiful big diamond she had just bought. The same thing goes for lovely clothes. A woman should have them, if she can earn them, while she's young, straight, graceful, slim, and can show them off like an angel.

Some working women do pay someone to help with the housework, and why shouldn't they if they dread the thought of scrubbing the kitchen floor after a day in the office? I feel a great sense of accomplishment, though, when I get down on my knees and scrub my own floor. When I spend months without doing a movie or a TV show and spend all my time at my desk or on a dais every night I have a lot of surplus energy to use up. Scrubbing, for me, is the greatest exercise in the world. It gives me rosy cheeks, and I just have a ball.

For the working couple, there are also ego factors involved. Bill's wife, Caroline, says that they used to go out of their way not to tell people she had a career. She happens to work under her maiden name, and she was aware that something can happen to a woman who gets very well known in her field. "She gets too independent. She overplays her professional role. She works harder, and neglects her husband."

Success can go to a woman's head probably faster than to a man's because she hasn't had it for as long as he. The man, on the other hand, wonders whether other people think his successful wife is dominating him and making all the decisions. He doesn't know, because no one tells him.

She doesn't know either! Do people consider her a dominating bitch? What are their roles as far as mutual friends are concerned? This calls for the most beautiful feminine tact. Any woman wants to make her husband happy, and a big part of that is letting him know that he is the boss, that it's his home, and his big comfortable world that they're living in. When they're together socially, she defers to him. She may have had the biggest success of her life that very morning, *but she doesn't mention it—* unless he does. And if he's as proud of her as he should be, he will. If he doesn't mention it, or plays it down, I think his insecurity is showing.

Women in some fields have a right to feel proud of their

achievements because, as Caroline says emphatically, "A woman has to be at least twice as good to be considered a success. Women have to work much harder than a man does just to get a modicum of success." This isn't always true. It isn't true in my business, as an actress or as a businesswoman. And it certainly isn't fair when it does happen. But thank goodness it's happening less and less.

I think we're all influenced, in the roles we play as men and women, by our parents. I've noticed lately in talking to successful career women that many of them mention their mother's achievements—in a day when very few women ever emerged from their own parlors. And men who take a strong position against their wives working are remembering gentle mothers whose whole lives were devoted to housekeeping—whether they liked it or not. Because then they didn't have a chance. And I'll bet a lot of them hated it!

A thing that a man will come back to, time and again, is whether the children are being neglected, or adversely affected. All the more reason for the parents to make it a happy home when they're all together, evenings and weekends.

"The most serious factor," Bill said, "is where children are involved. The working mother doesn't know how much time she's actually devoting to her family. The more successful she gets, the more involved she is in her job."

Caroline solved this by forming her own business so that she could work most of the time out of a room in her own house. But Bill persisted, "Even while she's working at home she has no actual way of determining how much attention she's giving to her children. Working in her room she might as well be miles away. Do the children feel shunted off?"

Probably no two people will ever agree on the exact amount of time a child should have with its parents. (I'll bet no two kids would agree, either!) For centuries the British have made a clear demarcation between a child's world and an adult's world. And

*With the twins—in their party dresses—at St. Moritz; below, in Nassau.*

it's worked. The children have their own activities during the day. They're played with and guided when they're toddlers, tutored as they grow older, and sent away to school, if the parents can afford it, before adolescence. When they're at home, they have their own hour downstairs with the family. It's all theirs. When they've learned to be civilized and not dribble cookies all over the rug they can come down for tea and join in the conversation. When they can handle a knife and fork nicely, at about seven or eight years of age, they can join the adults for dinner on special occasions.

But there's clearly their world, in the nursery, in the playground, and at school. They're happy that way. And the young English people I've met seem to mature earlier than our children. At eighteen they're suddenly grownup and polished and a pleasure to have around. Their relationships with their parents are warm and affectionate. They don't feel that they've been neglected, and they don't behave as if they've been overindulged.

As for me, I don't think a child really wants to live in an adult world, and it's a theory I've made work since I adopted my first daughter. It's the parents' job to transfer children gently out of their child's world and prepare them for growing up. But first we should go into their world and live there with them when they're young. When they start to reach for your world—and they'll want to when the right time comes—they'll know how to behave because they can trust you. They'll imitate you because they admire you.

Caroline took her two teenagers out to lunch and asked them frankly if they'd prefer it if she gave up her career. They were amazed at such a silly question. They *enjoyed* the fact that she worked—the daughter especially, who enjoys looking at her mother's dress designs and offering her opinion. They knew that when they needed her she was right there at her desk, or at the end of the telephone.

As Caroline says, "A working mother often has at least a part-time helper at home. Another person in the house helps to enlarge a small child's world."

Often there's no help in the home, but there are neighbors and friends and the people at nurseries and day-care centers. All of them help a child to learn to get along with all sorts of people and become more independent. Seeing people encourages him to make decisions for himself. When he sees his parents at his own special time of the day he enjoys them more than if they were underfoot all the time.

A man might wonder if the children of a successful woman might look upon her as the "father figure." How on earth could they, if their father is perfectly secure himself?

I've always thought, too, that "father" and "mother" are words that mean disciplinarian. I like the word "friend" instead. We wouldn't have, or adopt, children if we weren't anxious to be their greatest friends.

It's the quality of the time together that counts—not the number of waking hours.

I think I was a good mother. All of my four children were adopted, at the age of ten days, after I'd had a heartbreaking series of miscarriages. They understood that they were especially chosen, and I think they were rather pleased about it. Of course every woman tries to be a good mother, and then wonders if, after all her best efforts, her children will wind up on a head-shrinker's couch complaining about bad treatment.

I was strict about some things. The pediatrician told me that if all children took naps until they were twelve they'd be the healthiest ever. The kids hated that as they grew older, but it certainly paid off in good health.

They were taught the kind of self-sufficiency I'd had to learn in quite a different way when I was working my way through school. When they were old enough to stand on a stool at the sink they washed out their shoelaces and polished their little white shoes every day before putting them away. They hung up their clothes *if* they were clean—which wasn't very often.

But I didn't stand over them with a whip. If that kind of training is started early enough it becomes second nature. And it leaves you time to get on with more important things.

I was strict when I thought it was necessary, but I balanced it with tenderness, love, and plenty of my time. The children were brought onto the set when they were infants and all my spare moments were spent with them. They came to meet me in the evening and we drove home together and I had dinner with them. Our Sundays were precious. I took them to Sunday school and then there was a picnic or an outing in the afternoon.

Between every picture we would hit the road in the station wagon, the five of us and a medium-sized poodle. The twins rode in little homemade cribs that were tied on, so that when I drove they would rock as if they were in cradles. Christopher rode in the back, and Christina in front with me.

When feeding time came I'd say, "We're on a highway and I can't stop now. Christina, here are the warm bottles. You take one and give Christopher the other. Crawl over and the two of you feed the babies."

We often drove to Carmel on weekends and we loved walking along the shore. Christopher taught the little ones how to pick up the seashells and how, when the waves came in and washed out again, they'd find the tiny shells. I showed them how to pick out the most perfect ones and to hold them very gently so as not to crush them. We carried little baskets and there was a competition to see who could collect the most.

When I took the children to see the redwoods for the first time they stood in reverence. They couldn't even see the tops of the trees and they were awed when we drove right through them.

They were thrilled by the salmon run in Oregon. They had a taste of ranching at a place beyond Santa Barbara called Alisal Ranch. The head wrangler, Bill, used to lead both the twins' horses. Cathy loved horses, but the poor child was allergic to them and would come back with her eyes streaming. I finally found an allergy pill that helped until she outgrew it. Christina, until she was sixteen, wanted to be a cowboy. We went on pack trips, too. They were all wonderful adventures and, as usually happens in a large family, the big ones took awfully good care of the little ones.

We read a great deal of poetry together. I read aloud until they were able to, and then the older ones would read to the younger children. They loved the comic verses and cried over the sad ones. They wanted to hear *Mary Poppins* over and over. They couldn't get enough of the idea of her having tea on the ceiling. When Christina would giggle, then Christopher would chime in. And then Cindy and Cathy would burst out laughing even though they didn't know what they were laughing about.

They only responded, of course, to the things they really felt. They took those things into their souls, and still remember them today. The wonderful thing about poetry is that it articulates, in a beautiful way, what you've been feeling all along—and enlarges and explains the feeling.

I used to go out into the empty lots in Brentwood and play football with the kids. I taught my son and the three girls how to kick a football and how to pass and catch, and I think I had more fun than they did! I taught them swimming, riding, and tennis, ping-pong, and badminton.

On Halloween we'd all dress up, and when they were little I'd carry both twins, one on each hip, and the big kids would carry two bags each—one for each child. We'd play trick or treat at all the neighbors' houses and then, coming back up our little hill where we lived, Christopher and Christina would carry the babies on their backs. Some of our neighbors, Robert Preston, Barbara Stanwyck, and Jennings Lang and Monica Lewis among them, probably remember these Halloween visits. Cole Porter lived very near, too.

Another tradition was our Easter-egg hunt, with ice-cream cones afterward. I don't know who had more fun—the children or the mothers and fathers.

I discovered that I must have instilled a few of the social graces in the children when I let the twins take charge of their own ninth birthday party aboard the *Andrea Doria*. They invited the whole of the first class and decided on the menu by themselves. There was vodka and caviar, a clear soup, New York cut steak with a large selection of vegetables, a salad, and cheese trays— accompanied by a good red wine. Finally there was a tremendous birthday cake for all the guests, and Dom Perignon. I didn't suggest a bit of it to them. It was entirely their own menu.

I had often told them, "When you give someone something of your own, give the *best*." They learned that lesson only too well. On another Atlantic crossing that they made with their nurse, they were on the *Ile de France* when it rescued the passengers from the *Andrea Doria*. As soon as the twins woke up in the morning and heard that there were children on board without any clothes they handed over all their pretty lace-trimmed underthings. A beautiful gesture, but the recipients would probably have preferred warm wool coats.

I was a working mother, and making films is a time-consuming job, but I found time to expose the children to all facets of life, all sorts of experiences. They grew acquainted with the country, the mountains, the desert. They learned all sorts of sports to find out what they liked the best. Helen Hayes once said that the essential thing was to introduce children to life, and then let them make their own decisions.

They met all my friends and, on informal occasions, they'd join us at the dinner table in their highchairs. There were famous actors and great directors, but to the children they were just family friends. One day the twins were looking at television. After a few minutes they ran upstairs to where I was working and said indignantly, "Why didn't you tell us that Uncle Butch is Cesar Romero!"

But even when they realized that some of the family friends were world-famous they formed their own candid opinions of them, as children always do. They judged people in terms of whether they were kind, and related to them. They hated those who treated them like "little people" or, worse yet, as Joan Crawford's children. Kids are the wisest judges of all. They can instantly spot the difference between the way people act and what they really are.

Given all that exposure, they decided how their own lives would be. Christina decided to become an actress—and she's a damn good one. She'll be heard from, more and more.

*Christina's wedding party.*

The twins have never had any interest in the theater. Cindy, mother of two, is the wife of a successful farmer in Iowa. She was a born housewife and she always adored cooking. She'd beg to be allowed to help with our favorite Sunday picnic, fried chicken and potato salad, or to help make the hors d'oeuvres.

Cathy, who has one child, lives in the St. Lawrence Valley and helps her husband operate a large marina. He's a former naval officer and they're both in love with boats. In fact, they spent their honeymoon on one, sailing down the St. Lawrence and cooking their meals on a little hibachi. Cathy has considerable success with her painting, too—still-lifes and absolutely exquisite miniatures. Carleton Varney commissioned her to do seventy-five floral paintings for the Westbury Hotel in New York City, and other commissions come in faster than she can cope with them.

Both of my twins are a long way from Hollywood, but when they get together they reminisce about their childhood with, they assure me, a great deal of nostalgia. They tell people they had a marvelous childhood. I hope they all did. I tried to give them that—because it's really all that a parent can do. A parent has to guide, advise, educate, and love them. If they're sure of the love, they'll accept the guidance.

I think that children benefit in all sorts of ways when they have mothers who have their own fascinating jobs. It's good for them to know that mother is involved in other things besides smothering them with love. They respect that. When children are neglected it's usually because their mothers are so bored and discontented that they fill their days with golf, bridge, and matinees and leave the children to fend for themselves. A working woman loves coming home and making special time for her children. But few husbands understand the full range of her responsibilities.

A man works a five-day week and a seven- or eight-hour day—everyone should. But when the wife comes home she can't just sit down and relax. She has to see that the household is running beautifully. She must see that the maid has done everything she's expected to do, or do it herself, and that everything is in full supply—enough soap and light bulbs and vacuum-cleaner bags and all the other things a man thinks spring ready-made out of the cupboards.

She has to sort the laundry and see to the dry cleaning. Buy the groceries, plan the week's menus, and pay the household accounts. Arrange for entertaining. Somehow she has to squeeze in the time for her regular beauty routines, her visits to the hairdresser, and the replenishing of her own wardrobe. (Her husband expects her to look better than ever, doesn't he?)

She has to do all these things—and a few more—and pretend that some good angel is getting them done for her, because at the end of the day her "real" time belongs to her family. She has at least three full-time jobs to do—and two of them run seven days a week.

But all the women I've talked to agree that doing them keeps you young. Involved in things. And if husband and wife have both had a busy day and come back with a sense of achievement they can relax together in the evening. It takes a man off the hook about having to entertain his wife or keep her interested in things. She isn't dependent on him to relieve her of boredom, because she hasn't got time to be bored.

Ideally, a woman should take a job that leaves her time somewhat flexible. A full-fledged career woman can manage this. And many women taking more ordinary jobs arrange to skip their lunch hour so that they can be home by four. Then mother can be there when everyone else arrives. She's had time to freshen herself and make sure that everything looks relaxed and inviting.

Basically, there are two situations:

1. She was a career woman before marriage and wants to continue. They discuss it and arrive at reasonable areas of agreement about children and finances.

2. She wants to resume a career—or begin one—now that the children are growing up.

In the first case I think that a couple should have rather a long engagement. In fact I'm firmly in favor of people knowing each other well—even living together—before they get married. It's the only way they can get to know each other as well as they should. Divorce is a very messy and unpleasant business, and it's always a very painful one. Someone feels rejected. There is no worse feeling in the world, and it takes a lot of healing, especially for people who haven't learned to adjust, compromise, be resilient. Those are the ones who suffer the most.

Dating, even having an affair, is an artificial situation. It's still a romance, with both on their best behavior. But is this the way they're going to be in marriage? Aren't they likely to get sloppy, careless, inconsiderate? How will they react to outside demands on their time? How will two careers bear up under the strain?

It's not always a matter of making sure that a man is willing to have a working wife. Sometimes it's the other way around. I know a man who married a very successful career woman because that's the kind of woman he admired and was attracted to. Not many months later she quit her job and announced her intention of becoming a suburban matron. He had chosen a woman who was involved and interesting—and became the most uninteresting woman in the world. Poor man!

I know of another beautiful and very much sought-after woman who didn't marry until she was thirty-eight. Because none of the men who fell in love with this charming blonde would agree to her carrying on her business, and she could conceive of no other way of life. She wanted to marry. She is completely feminine. But her work was fascinating, and it was the other half of her. It fulfilled her.

I have a happy ending to that story. She met a very attractive and successful man who wanted her exactly as she was. As in the case of the Lunts, he realized that she was no housekeeper. They decorated a lovely little penthouse, hired a woman to do the cleaning, and when she comes home every evening he is waiting for her with a well-chilled bottle of wine and some caviar or pâté. They're blissfully happy.

When a woman wants to go back to work after some years of marriage, there is, as I said, a lot of tact required. She's doing it, probably, because her world suddenly seems empty and meaningless. Physically she's youthful, still very attractive. But her mind seems vacant of anything but the memory of diapers and PTA meetings. She senses that there's an exciting world outside the garden gate and she wants to be part of it.

She'll have to rely a good deal on her knowledge of her husband's psychology. Maybe she'll have to convince him that her sudden desire to leap over the garden gate doesn't mean that she wants another man. Maybe she'll have to protect his ego from the idea that he isn't providing for her well enough.

One good tactic, if she senses problems ahead, is to start cultivating friendships with other working couples, so that her husband will say to himself, "Tom is a pretty lucky guy! His wife is an interesting gal with a good job—and she still takes good care of him!"

Most men soon find that a career wife contributes more than an extra pay check. Women submerged in a domestic situation are often at sea in general company. Women in the business world learn how to develop a tact and ease that is a great asset to a man socially. This has nothing to do with basic talent or education. It's a matter of meeting many different kinds of people and handling all sorts of situations in daily life. A working wife is able to entertain his friends and business associates much more confidently because she understands their world. She's flexible with strangers because she has learned to be flexible in her own life. She's interesting, easy to talk to, and contributes to both the social and the business scene.

The boss will say, "You know, Jim's wife is quite a woman, isn't she? Handles people well. I wonder whether we shouldn't consider him for that vacancy coming up in public relations? That involves a lot of entertaining, and the right wife is important."

This is a side benefit, and not a minor one. The major benefit is that working is the best way of being completely fulfilled. And that's the kind of woman who makes her husband happiest.

During my little research into the special problems of working couples I talked to my old friends, Lynn and Alfred Lunt—perhaps the most famous (and blissfully married) professional pair in the world. Many audiences wonder if after smiling adoringly at each other at the final curtain they rush out to the wings to bicker over who got the best notices, or whether she has to hurry home to prepare supper.

Nothing could be further from the truth with the Lunts. Lynn says, quite bluntly, "I'm not a housekeeper and he knew that when he married me, and so he couldn't complain. As a matter of fact he did the housekeeping and very often all the cooking. He's a wonderful cook."

As for professional conflicts, she said, "We're both working people, you know. Do you suppose that while I was studying O'Neill's *Mourning Becomes Electra* and he was doing *Marco*

*Millions,* there was *time* to indulge in any grousing? Perhaps that is the mysterious secret of our happy marriage—or one of them. That there was no time."

She added, "I'm not a jealous woman, which is a wonderful thing, both for me and for him."

I've rarely met two people who are more compatible. They agree on how their lovely house in Wisconsin should be kept, and Alfred oversees its management, although Lynn says, "If we're having guests I go to each of the rooms and see that everything's perfect, enough towels and if anything is dusty, you know. I'm good at that. We're very lucky to have Jules, who's been with us for a lifetime and who is now the major-domo of the house and sees that everything is all right.

"We do the decorating together. Alfred has painted several rooms, and I did one bedroom entirely. He painted the hall and stairway. We agree on color. We agree a good deal about anything to do with art. On that kind of thing we agree absolutely."

There are two good secrets that came out of that conversation:

A working couple hasn't *time* for "grousing."

And there are large areas of complete agreement.

Each couple has to find its own formula. For some, complete honesty is the approach—being able to sit down and talk things out—and the ability to make compromises. It's important to be very close for the short time that's available in a busy day or a busy week, to make that hour totally concentrated, important, precious.

Sure it takes an effort. Some people seem to feel that everything should be instantaneous—like freeze-dried coffee. But usually it takes hard work, and a good deal of tact.

Once a man is convinced that his creature comforts—and his sex life—are going to be taken care of, and that the children won't be "neglected," he'll start thinking happily that the second pay check will enable you both to make that trip to Europe, or to buy a cottage in the country, or to make a better education possible for the children.

He'll wind up being very proud of you and I'll bet there'll be something like a second honeymoon. As for you—you'll come alive!

## ·VI·

## Moving into a Man's World

IT's *how* you move into it that counts! Men who are prejudiced against women in executive positions have usually had a bad experience with one who swaggered in with a chip on her manly shoulder believing that she had to *fight* her way up, and fight men to do it. A gal like that can make it tough for the rest of us. Many in the women's liberation movement have done that—but few of them are executives and few are very good to look at. They have nothing to lose but their uncombed hair.

The fact is, there are many women in top management and they're not wearing mannish suits and sensible shoes, *or* chips on their shoulders. They're wearing stunning clothes with good labels, their hair and skin have an expensive, well-cared-for look, they glow with health because they take good care of their bodies, and they sparkle with fresh ideas.

I meet them at conventions, I join them on the dais, I lunch with them, and I find them always stimulating, and invariably feminine. One of my dearest friends, Mary Roebling, was the first woman to become president and now board chairman of a major bank. There is no more feminine and charming person alive. A woman who has succeeded magnificently in a man's world, she is always treated like a lady—simply because that's what she expects.

There should be no confusion about manners, she says: "A lady is treated like a lady by a gentleman—because he is a gentleman." Even if they are both vice presidents.

117

## My Way of Life

I never dreamed, when I danced my way into pictures, that one day I'd be a "lady executive." I think I would have been horrified at the idea. But life keeps springing nice surprises. As a director of a large corporation I'm having as much fun now as I ever did in those crazy Black Bottom-and-Charleston days when Scott Fitzgerald called me "the best example of the flapper."

*Travel is a big part of my way of life. Into my traveling suit, off to the airport, paperwork en route (with Mamacita next to me), and then the arrival at another Pepsi bottling plant.*

People in the business world are like any other people—amusing, warm, generous, stimulating—and the most loyal friends. Men have great respect for a woman who can be both competent and attractive. Competence without charm can irritate some men. I think you should be appealing, but not in a phony way. It has to be part of your personality. If it isn't, acquire it, and they'll forgive your know-how. After all, men really love women more than they hate them!

I never try to compete as a man. Like all women, I have a special contribution to make to the business world. Women do most of the purchasing in this country. They understand quality and value, and appreciate attractive packaging because they know how to package themselves! Any woman who thinks she'd

*On a business trip to San Antonio I was presented with a stuffed dik-dik—a fully grown deerlike animal that has been specially bred in Africa for its miniature size.*

be lost in business, or lacking in valuable ideas, should just try it. She can bring ideas to industry that men have never dreamed of. "The Power of a Woman" is a cliché—but one with a foundation, and I don't mean a girdle. A woman can make her family consume anything she buys if it's attractively packaged. They'll acquire a taste for it if mother says so.

But she must be tactful, feel her way. With certain men, you have to make them think it's their idea. With others, if you know your job and you've proved your capability, you can come right out and present your own ideas. But tact, after all, isn't a thing that operates exclusively between men and women. It exists between *people,* based on consideration and a great love of people, an ability to put yourself in someone else's position, to understand. It takes a lot of doing to acquire tact, but it's the essential oil that smoothes every human relationship. You even have to be tactful with your own children!

No working relationship can be based on the premise, "Me—woman; you—man!" It's "we two" trying to make a job better.

When I'm working on a picture, if a scene goes wrong in rehearsal I say, "There's something wrong with this—it goes wrong right here."

It happened not long ago, and Robert Gist, the director, said, "I know, I feel it every time when you get to that one line."

"Let's try it again," I said, "and let me try it as it comes to me that the character, Marion, would do it." I played around with different things in the rehearsals and then suddenly I said, "I've got it! Let's shoot, let's get it on film, because I may never be able to recapture that one brief second again."

We printed that scene.

Where the tact came in was in my referring to the character, and what the script had said earlier that *she* would do. I didn't say, "This is what a woman would do," or, "This is what I, Joan Crawford, think should be done."

121

*Performing takes another beautiful chunk of my time. Within a recent year I did a cameo with Robert Vaughn and David McCallum in "The Man From U.N.C.L.E.," starred in an episode of "The Virginian" with James Drury, and made a full-length film in London, Trog.*

*Checking my makeup before doing a TV commercial.*

You have to be fond of men to work with them. I don't mean to the point of falling in love with them every five minutes, but genuinely liking and respecting them and wanting to be friends with them. But that can't be forced. It should come slowly, naturally. Every now and then I'll think, "That person just rubs me the wrong way. There's a personality conflict." A year later he may turn out to be my best friend—and I mean friend in the real sense. There's a chemistry with friendship, just as with lovers, that has to be left alone to work in its own way.

Mary Roebling showed me the results of a questionnaire that went out to male American banking executives asking them how they felt about women in their field. "Women," said the male bankers, "must get away from using the multitude of feminine techniques and wiles to climb the ladder to business success."

It's amazing that there really *are* men who think we're going to slink into their offices dressed like Mata Hari and drenched with musky perfume! They must be leading very sheltered lives.

Most of the bankers also felt that women are more emotional, less stable, than men.

Not true! I think by nature a woman is *more* stable. Life gives her so many different things to cope with, and she learns almost from infancy to cope and not to let it show. A woman who has married and brought up children has had a thousand emergencies —illnesses, broken plumbing, appliances refusing to operate, the children's naughtiness, her husband's moods, the bills—and has trained herself to take them all in stride.

A man has his regular working routine, with assistants and secretaries to take on a lot of the headaches, and usually at the end of the day he can forget about the shop and relax.

Those bankers think that women's feelings are more easily hurt, that they can't take the same hard knocks that men must in the business world, that they tend to take criticism personally. Sure, women can be hurt—more than men. But a man's ego is a very fragile thing, and many a husband has come home and said, "You know, the boss just doesn't *like* me!" If a woman came home and said that her husband would probably reply, "Well, I'm glad he doesn't like you—that much!"

People ask me if I turn up at board meetings wearing tailored costumes in muted colors. Oh no, I say. I wear hot and shocking pink and lovely hats. I don't think any man ever did a poor job because he had an attractively dressed woman to look at. In fact, the sight probably challenges him to be his most brilliant self. But when it comes to the routine of the meeting I do exactly what the men do. I raise my hand. They say, "Yes, Joan?" And I give them my idea, or ask them to expand on theirs.

Thecla Haldane is a free-lance photographer who has been

working for Pepsi, and with me, for about ten years and who knows more than most of us about working in a man's world. There are only half a dozen Theclas flying around the world in jet aircraft covering news events and wars along with thousands of male photographers.

She's worked in Korea, Vietnam, the Belgian Congo, Liberia, Alaska, and dozens of spots in between. She was the only woman on a battleship with President De Gaulle, she's covered three American Presidents, flown in Air Force One, and photographed most of the crowned heads still left in the world. Her formula is, "Conduct yourself like a lady, and you're always treated like one." She's never "one of the boys." Sometimes, on rough assignments in war zones, or when the temperature's twenty below, she has to dress as the men do. But whenever possible she wears a lovely dress. She's suitably dressed for every occasion she covers, from a party for Haile Selassie to a White House banquet.

She says, "If my male opposite is secure in his job I never have any trouble with him. No jealousy, no problems. It's the insecure ones trying to get a leg up who are difficult." That's probably true in any business.

One of the things a woman has to handle in business is taking men out to lunch. In industry you must entertain customers, in public relations you must invite editors. At a certain level it's an essential part of the job, but most men feel very uneasy about being a woman's guest in a restaurant.

The hostess should never, of course, handle money. It's even awkward to use a credit card because the waiter has to bring the bill, she has to quickly figure out the tip and write it in, and sign it. When possible, I take along a male colleague from my office and he signs the check. But the best system of all is to establish an understanding with one or two good restaurants, open charge accounts, and have the bills—with tips added—sent to your office. When a business lunch is finished I glance around and say, "Would anybody like another cup of coffee?" If no one does, that's my signal to get up, and we all leave. A man can't be embarrassed if it's handled this way.

When there are only four or six of us we have menus, and knowing my favorite restaurants, Chauveron and "21," so well, I usually mention one or two of their specialties. It helps the ordering to go quickly. If there are more than six I usually order by phone earlier in the day, and as my guests arrive a waiter will whisper to them what the main dish is so that they can, if they wish, ask for something else.

For a party of ten or twelve who are all going to be discussing a given topic—and this often happens with the charities I'm involved with—I like to ask for a private room. I don't think people can speak freely in such a large group in an open restaurant, and I'm sure it bothers the other customers.

With a private room, a bar is set up, and for half an hour we circulate while we're having our drinks and something to munch on, and introduce people who haven't met before. This is almost as warm and friendly as entertaining in your own home—and no cleaning up to do afterward.

While we're still on the subject of restaurants, I must register one prejudice of mine: lady table-hoppers. I think there is *nothing* more undignified than a woman who flits around greeting everyone she knows—and probably interrupting someone else's business talk. She can smile across the room if she recognizes a friend, and let him stop at *her* table on the way out if he has time.

As for the other little amenities—yes, the lady lets the man light her cigarette, help her on with her coat, and open the door for her. Even if he's the boss. Manners are manners, and success doesn't mean that a woman has to forgo the courtesies that make life easy and pleasant.

*Above, lunching at Chauveron with Norman N. Coates, Mrs. Donald Sills, and Frederick P. Pro to plan the next Muscular Dystrophy Ball. Below, doing a telethon for Muscular Dystrophy. Opposite top, I was privileged to share a dais with Mrs. Lyndon B. Johnson in her Keep America Beautiful campaign. Opposite bottom, Frances Spingold and I helped with the Heart Ball in Palm Beach. She is responsible for the Theatre Arts Center at Brandeis University, in one wing of which is the Joan Crawford Dance Studio.*

*At my desk.*

*Helping Maurice Chevalier celebrate the publication of his lovely new book.*

*Above, at an American Cancer Society affair with guess-what-famous violinist. Below, receiving one of the first awards to the Ten Outstanding Woman in Business, voted by 500 newspaper and magazine editors throughout the country.*

In an office, being feminine doesn't mean being seductive. Not that there isn't plenty of seduction in the business world. It's getting more rare these days, I think, to find men and women who are merely friends. But if you're keeping a good marriage going you won't need any office flirtations—and you certainly won't have any time left over for an affair. Besides, it's very poor strategy. Even a flirtation, when it wears off, causes some bad feeling, and somebody is going to be moved into another department—or out of the company. Quite likely you!

There are no hard-and-fast rules for fending off an outright pass, especially if it comes from the boss. Every intelligent woman has her own method of turning it off without wounding a sensitive male ego. An even cleverer woman knows how to prevent the pass

*Tea at 10 Downing Street with Prime Minister and Mrs. Harold Wilson and Sir Billy Butlin, during my long stay in London in 1960.*

*In the famous oval office. I had a thirty-minute chat with the late President Kennedy.*

in the first place. She's charming, friendly, capable—and not seductive. If you can't control your cleavage, your perfume, your walk, and your eyelashes—you'd better stay out of business. Your husband will worry enough about the thought that other men are finding you attractive during the day, and it will spark your marriage if he does. But he'll sense it instantly if something really is going on.

Good jobs can't always be squeezed in from nine to five. Mine certainly isn't. If your husband is used to a rigid schedule you'll have to wean him away from it gradually. It's not too difficult to fit the demands of a career around a satisfying private life. Maybe you've always dined with the Joneses on Thursday evening. Now, sometimes, there's a late meeting or even a trip. Of course you don't let him think that you love the late hours or out-of-town sales conferences, but as he's a businessman himself, he can see that sometimes they're necessary.

Persuade him that life *shouldn't* be lived by a rigid schedule. Life should be flexible, to allow for extra work sometimes—and extra fun at other times. A hard week may rate a long weekend, an unpremeditated flight to the islands for a miniature honeymoon! A rigid schedule makes me suspect insecurity of some kind. Flexibility is mature. It leaves room for surprises—nice ones.

Many women really need that flexibility in their jobs, especially when their children are small and making more demands on them. Until they're teenagers and on their own it may be necessary to settle for a part-time job. More and more employers are realizing that a mature woman can get more done in a four- or five-hour day than a boy-crazy girl can in seven hours with coffee breaks. So more and more of these jobs are becoming available.

Many enterprising women start small businesses out of their own homes. This isn't really getting out into the world, but it can bring a tiny portion of the world to your door. Libraries are crammed with books on small businesses tailored for women who can't free themselves completely—and they bear looking into.

I've heard of women who started beauty parlors in a spare room, or thrift shops, or who took courses to become real-estate brokers. Others have special talents or college training that they can put to use on a part-time basis. Any woman can start a child-care center.

You may not start at the board-room table, but you *can* start— somewhere. And a great big new world will open up.

# ·VII·

## Four Miles High with Fifteen Suitcases

I'VE FLOWN more than three million miles for Pepsi. No, I don't *hate* flying, but I'm always very happy when we land. There's something unnatural about spending so much time suspended 30,000 feet above the earth.

Not many women have jobs calling for such mobility, but I'm Pepsi's good-will ambassador, and one of my main activities is attending the opening of bottling plants all over the world. In addition, I fly to business conventions and the meetings of any number of charitable organizations, and I fly to my film and TV jobs. In one frantic period last year I flew to London to make a movie, came back and covered twelve cities for Pepsi, flew out to California to do *The Virginian,* had five days in New York, went back to the Coast for the final work on a movie, came home for three days, spent ten days in Brazil for Pepsi, and then did twelve more cities.

At every pause in the schedule I fell flat on my face. The time lag destroys me. It takes me forty-eight hours to recover on overseas travel. Recently Lowell Thomas was congratulated on looking so well and someone asked him how he did it. He said, "My doctor told me to just stop crossing the date line too often."

The night flights—and so often those are the only ones available for long trips like the ones to South America—are very rough because I don't sleep on a plane. So my schedule is arranged so that I can fall into bed as soon as I arrive and sleep around the clock. My maid and the Pepsi girl who travel with me feel the jolt as much as I do. We are three very collapsible women after one of those long hops.

It's a joke at Pepsi that I'd rather drive, and that I don't let the chauffeur go more than forty-five miles an hour, even when there's a motorcycle escort. It's true. I know the driver goes mad, and so do the trucks behind us, but I'm not in that much of a hurry. And as a matter of fact I get a lot of work done on a long car trip. Also I get a chance to see the countryside closely enough almost to reach out and touch the trees. Sometimes we take our lunch and stop at the side of the road with it—chicken, cherry tomatoes, and hard-boiled eggs are a favorite picnic.

But when fly we must, there are always rewarding experiences at the other end. I travel to countries where I can't even spell the name of the language, but I've never encountered a communications barrier. I think that in learning to understand so many roles as an actress I've learned to understand all kinds of people. I can reach out to them because I really want to know them, and I've never been disappointed in their response.

I learn to say some gracious thing in each language. In Brazil it was a phrase that meant, "I embrace you." Learning at least one gracious phrase in the host country's language is the easiest applause-getter there is—and the fastest way of making friends. I'm usually offered some gift as a memento (in Texas a ten-gallon hat, in Wisconsin, cheese), but I had to refuse the kind offer of my hosts in Brazil: they wanted to give me a wildcat to take home with me.

The welcome in São Paulo was almost too much. There were thousands of people on the street, pressing in on the little Impala (the largest car in Brazil) until it began rocking. It was frightening—though it was very flattering, and very exciting.

It was a business trip to São Paulo, Brazil, to open a Pepsi bottling plant. But it was carnival time too, and I had a ball. Above, with the Cardinal and the Governor.

*Dancing with the entertainers at the São Paulo Pepsi plant opening.*

Even the friendliest crowds can be terrifying. One day in a department store so many people pressed forward to shake my hand that they pushed us against a counter, and Sharon Crane, who was with me, still shudders when she thinks of how close we came to going through the plate-glass counter.

On the sleepless plane flights I always love talking to the stewardesses. They bring me meal after meal until I cry for mercy, and sometimes we play gin rummy. One time I played it with Thecla on the way out to the airport. We wanted to finish the game so I said, "Come along!" She hopped aboard and we finished on the way to Washington.

Of course she had no luggage with her, but she went into her room and showered and was getting ready for bed when I had some unexpected guests in my sitting room. I phoned her to come and join us. In a few minutes she did, but she looked uncomfortable, and I couldn't understand why, for almost an hour of conversation, she refused to sit down. After the guests had left she explained the catastrophe. She had washed out her girdle. When I called her she'd put it back on, very damp, and she couldn't risk the dampness coming through her linen dress. Funny now, but not much fun for her at the time.

On another Washington trip we had one of our very rare small disasters. Our plane was early and there was no one at the airport to meet us. It was late at night so we commandeered three taxis and Mamacita and Sharon Crane and I each took one and divided the luggage out among us.

Halfway into town, in the middle of a bridge, one of the cabs broke down. Right then and there, at midnight, we transferred the baggage again and, sitting on each other's laps, managed to get to the hotel. Heading down the corridor to our rooms we had another short delay. From one of the doors came the shouts of a dozen teenage girls having a pajama party.

I stopped and knocked. After a long minute the door opened cautiously. A little girl peered out and then her mouth dropped open.

"Ohmygod, ohmygod, it's Joan Crawford!" she screamed.

There must have been almost two dozen girls there, wearing sweatshirts over their pajamas and all jumping up and down on the beds screaming and looking for their cameras. So I posed with them, signed autographs, and phoned the manager to ask him to send up several cases of Pepsi and some Fritos. One of the girls dashed down the hall to fetch the nuns who were chaperoning them, and they joined the party cheerfully.

A trip for Pepsi is almost as carefully organized as a moon shot. It begins when the girl who accompanies me gets a request from a bottler proposing a date for the opening of the plant. If it fits into my schedule she goes on in advance to meet the bottler and his family and brings back the material on the size of the plant, how long it's been in operation, if at all, before the official opening, and all the other business details. She is the field man. She knows what the schedule is to be—press conferences, receptions, the invocation—and briefs me. Then she checks on our accommodations and transportation. Bob Kelly trained the girls and men who have traveled with me—and did it brilliantly. They never make a mistake.

Trips in the United States are usually planned for a weekend so that the local families can participate. We arrive on Thursday night. There's an unofficial reception at the airport and then we go straight to the hotel or motel reserved for us.

On Friday interviews are scheduled for the press, then television, then local radio. Our main press conference is held when Pepsi's Chairman and/or President arrives, and we're joined by the bottler. That evening a banquet is preceded by a reception. We stand on the receiving line with the bottler and his wife and sometimes the governor or the mayor for an hour and a half. Promptly at eight the lights blink and we go in to dinner. Dinner is timed so that the speeches are over and the plaques presented by ten on the button, and I'm off to my hotel.

When I get there I have to pack because all the luggage has to be out at seven-thirty. In the morning, I arrive at the plant at ten. At ten-ten we have the invocation, at ten-fifteen platform guests and speakers are introduced, at ten forty-five we start touring the plant, and from eleven to twelve I'm on a platform, autographing. On the dot of noon I head for the airport.

This is the way things are scheduled in pictures, and it's why I like everything scheduled down to the second. It's been my training.

Unfortunately, I have no control over the timing of the charitable functions I attend—but oh, how I wish I did! When I'm to make a speech at ten, it's a long wait if I have to be there at six-thirty, stand around for two hours, and sit through a long dinner and many, many speeches waiting for my turn. Many people in my position feel that way. We're so glad to make appearances for charity, but it would be easier on us if the affairs could be a little bit briefer, a little bit better organized.

Recently I stood on a receiving line from six-thirty until eight-thirty and *then* crowds of new people started arriving and we didn't manage to get back to my rooms for a quiet dinner until almost ten.

Another of my problems in public life is the cigar-smoking male. A haze of cigar smoke—and one stogie can create as big a haze as four—renders me almost helpless. Sometimes at a banquet the most honored guest, sitting right next to me, is the one to pull out one of these Churchillian monsters, light up, and puff happily away for forty minutes. I wave feebly to my friends at another table and disappear behind the smoke screen.

The Pepsi team takes care of all my scheduling, but I have to organize my packing. It's a time-consuming job, and no amount of practice makes it go any faster. First I look at my itinerary—a recent trip to Copenhagen is a good example.

Well, to begin with there was one of my dreaded night flights—and it was in warm weather. I needed a dark, nonwrinkling costume for the plane that would look presentable when I was met at the airport the following morning.

The next day I needed something tailored for a press conference, and then had to make a quick change for a fashion show.

For the third day I needed a chiffon dress for a luncheon at the Royal Yacht Club. And on my last day I needed a long dress

*During my 1970 trip to Copenhagen, with Hans Vieth and Norman Heller.*

for a dinner party at the home of our plant manager and his wife, Mr. and Mrs. Hans Vieth.

It happened that there was such a heat wave during my week in Copenhagen that I didn't leave the hotel except for these events, and for a visit to the plant and to the Tivoli Gardens. But not knowing about the heat wave, I had packed three costumes to wear sightseeing, exploring the city or going down that enchanting "walking street." I love looking into shop windows and buying impulsively when I have the chance.

In addition to what I would wear in Copenhagen I packed for a long homeward trip via Paris and the *S.S. France.* I hadn't had a vacation in eight years and I was determined to get those five days at sea to sleep and read and sleep and read. This meant several more traveling dresses and things suitable for shipboard —although I was enjoying my rest and quiet so much that I only went up to the dining room once. That was for the gala night at the captain's table. To my pleasure Lilly Daché and her husband were there and it was so good to see her. We had worked together for years.

For all my trips, before getting my suitcases and hatboxes up from the storage room I make a list of the number and kinds of costumes I'll need and then go through my closets. I never remember when I've last worn a dress and the hemline may not be right. I try on everything to make sure it fits perfectly. I already know that it's spotless because nothing goes back into the closet until it is. Sometimes new things have to be ordered, so my inventory starts well in advance of a big trip.

I can't anticipate everything I'll need. I can't predict the weather—it can change suddenly. I may find there's no air conditioning. Or that the ladies will be wearing something different from what I'd expected. So I have to have alternatives with me.

I always pack in daylight. In artificial light when I'm in a hurry it's too easy to grab the wrong accessories and find myself in Kansas City or San Juan with a hot pink dress and a shocking pink hat—and that's a catastrophe.

I try to aim for versatility when I order clothes. I like reversible coats, for instance. One side may be dark gray, the other light gray. In the same fabrics I have both light and dark gray gloves and handbags. With the dark side of the coat out I'll wear a light gray dress with white accents. With the other side I'll wear a dark gray dress with red polka dots. This gives me two ensembles in less space.

I always have two skirts made for my cocktail dresses—one

short and one long. I can wear the short one to a reception, then fly back to my room and put on the long one for the formal dinner.

I love preshrunk cottons for traveling. Mamacita can wash and press them overnight—another space-saving trick. Whatever I've worn that day goes into the hotel bathtub for a good soak and some squishing back and forth, and then after a time Mamacita goes in and rinses them, rolls them in big towels, and irons them while they're still damp.

Packing days are pretty hectic. My work still goes on. The phone keeps ringing. The dictation has to be done. But at every pause I'm back in the bedroom making selections, having try-ons, and collecting all the accessories. When I have six or eight outfits assembled I say to Mamacita, "Let's pack these projects, right here."

The dresses are put into the suitcases on their hangers, with the gloves pinned to them, still in their plastic bags. The accessories are placed right next to the dresses they go with. I'm probably one of America's biggest consumers of tissue paper. It's folded between the dresses and into the sleeves and stuffed into shoes and handbags. My hats are stuffed with tissue, encased in plastic bags, and packed into large black drums that hold perhaps a dozen—drums about three feet high and almost too wide to get through the door of my apartment or into a car. But we always manage. And there is just no other way to transport lovely hats.

At the end, Mamacita and I have twelve to fifteen pieces of luggage between us—mostly mine. On arrival, everything is whisked out and hung up. I make my first change, and I'm off to work. I'll say, "Mamacita, I'll be back in an hour and a half. Be sure the blue outfit with all the accessories is ready to put on when I return."

*Packing for a trip. I choose the dresses and assemble all the accessories on my bed. Mamacita stuffs the sleeves with tissue so that they won't wrinkle.*

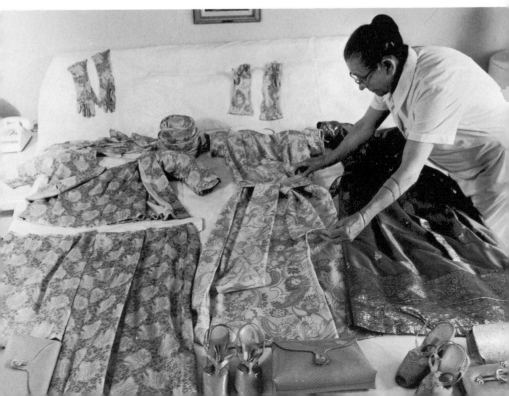

*My hats go into their own boxes. The cases are so big that the final assembling is usually done in the hall.*

## Four Miles High with Fifteen Suitcases

When I went to London to make *Trog* I had thirty-seven pieces of luggage. This isn't sheer vanity. I study the script carefully and get a feeling for what the character should wear. I select several outfits for each scene. But the producer is the final judge. He knows what color is right, and whether a dress is too busy for a dramatic scene, or for a certain set. We test all the clothes before shooting begins so we don't make any mistakes.

In the privacy of my own home my tastes are very simple. Working, I wear a cotton shift, usually pink, and a pair of ninety-eight-cent rubber pool sandals because my polished parquet floors are slippery and I've broken several ankles in my time. (I've even had to travel with one.) But the dresses are crisp and pretty and even for a morning at my desk I'm well enough groomed to receive any unexpected visitors.

In a public relations job like mine, though, a large and varied wardrobe is part of what people expect. I give it to them, along with my eagerness to make friends with all of them.

# ·VIII·

## Applause...and Solitude

I LOVE PEOPLE. I've been asked if I ever go around in disguise. Never! I think disguise is corny. If you've earned a position, be proud of it. Don't hide it. I want to be recognized. When I hear people say, "There's Joan Crawford!" I turn around and say, "Hi! How are you?"

It's a lovely feeling. You see, people in the theater get their applause after each act. In movies, we never hear it. Being recognized in public is our applause and it's silly to pretend not to enjoy it—and to feel very grateful for it.

Greta Garbo is a sad exception to this feeling. I think she's missed a great deal, and I'm sorry. I adore this woman—I have tremendous admiration for her, and tremendous compassion. We had dressing rooms next to each other for seventeen years at M-G-M. It was the greatest joy of my life when I heard we were going to make a picture together—*Grand Hotel.* But we had no scenes together. Every morning as I passed her door I'd say timidly, "Good morning, Miss Garbo." She never replied. I would scuttle shyly past to the set. Finally, one morning, I gave up. I didn't say anything. That day she came out of her dressing room and said brightly, "Gud morrning!"

This broke the ice—or at least made a slight crack in it. She was finally persuaded, five years later, by George Cukor to come and have tea with me in my portable dressing room. I had my best dishes out and the tea was brewing and I told Richard Bole-slavsky, the director, "Now when she comes over, you'll have to take a break or shoot somebody else's close-ups—because I wouldn't miss this meeting for anything in the world."

She came in, very timidly, and looked around. It happened that I had the only dressing room with a john, so my opening remark to this magical person was, "I have a john. Do you?"

"No!" she said. "Where?"

I opened it up and pulled the little seat out.

"Oh," she said, "that's luvvly, luvvly!" in that wonderful deep voice of hers. Friends, then, we had our tea. But I never saw her again.

Perhaps Miss Garbo isn't lonely, as so many people think, but has learned to use solitude. It can be so valuable as a time to grow, and to perceive things with all your senses. To read, and to take a measure of yourself and know where you're going, and why. I cherish the times—and they're rare—when I can lock the doors, turn off the phones, and settle down with my dogs at my feet and Mamacita hovering somewhere in the background.

I think it's time to explain that Mamacita isn't a Spanish girl, she's a German lady who raised nine children and has many grandchildren.

I took a house in Westhampton nine or ten years ago—a place to take the children for the summer. I had no one to help me and I didn't want to spend two months making beds and scrubbing bathrooms. I called a neighbor who put his maid on the phone. "I know someone for you," she said. "But I don't know whether you can put up with her. She's never heard of a bucket and a mop."

"Handsies, kneesies?" I asked.

"Yep," she replied.

"Bring her over tomorrow morning. That's just my cup of

tea. I never did think you could get into corners with any mop. Who is it?"

"My mother," she said. "I'll bring her."

The next morning I was on the phone when they arrived. I turned for a moment and said, "Start in my bedroom and have her work her way through the other bedrooms and then down here," and then I went back to the phone. When I hung up I wanted to call her to come quickly to take the dogs out but I realized that I hadn't asked her name. I had just returned from Rio de Janeiro, where all I had heard was mamacita, papacita, cousincita, everythingcita, so without thinking I called out, "Mamacita!"

Back she cried, "Ya! Ich comming!"

The name has stuck ever since. In all the countries we have traveled to together, in all languages, everyone calls her Mamacita.

We had language problems for a while, and it gave me the best exercise I've ever had in pantomime. I had to act out everything I wanted her to do, speaking slowly and distinctly about each action, each idea. I'd say, "Guest, lady, this room. One bed only."

She'd watch my mouth carefully, then watch my elaborate little scene. Finally a beautiful smile of comprehension would spread over her face and she'd say, "Oh, ya! Ya! Ich do!"

Inevitably, when we're traveling, she's referred to as my mother.

"What would your mother like to drink, Miss Crawford?"

"Gin and tonic, please."

She'll giggle and nudge me, very pleased. "He thinks I'm ya mama!" I let it go. I don't know what I'd do without Mamacita. No new situation ever flusters her. And new situations turn up every day.

People ask me if being a businesswoman conflicts with my acting, or vice versa. Not at all. One helps the other. The one has prepared me for the other—and both are preparing me for something else. What it is, I don't know. But if I learn from that past experience, then I'm going to be ready. Maybe there's a completely different career coming up, though I wouldn't dream of giving up the old ones entirely. I'll soon make my eighty-sixth film and I'm just as excited about it as I was about my first or my tenth. I was given faith in God, a strong, healthy body, and drive, and they all work together.

Bill Haines describes me as a many-faceted human being. My only regret is that because of the parts I've played in movies and on television people never expect me to have a sense of humor. I'd like to say, "Look, I can be funny, too!" But I can't hit them over the head with it. I don't take myself seriously, but I do take my work seriously. I love changing pressure into a challenge, and enjoying it.

I seek peace, too. I'll never sit back and vegetate, but I cherish peace of mind. I love the lines that were written by Max Ehrmann, the Indiana poet and lawyer. He calls them "Desiderata."

> Go placidly amid the noise and the haste, and remember what peace there may be in silence. As far as possible, without surrender, be on good terms with all persons. Speak your truth quietly and clearly; and listen to others, even to the dull and the ignorant; they too have their story. Avoid loud and aggressive persons; they are vexatious to the spirit. If you compare yourself with others, you may become vain or bitter, for always there will be greater and lesser persons than yourself. Enjoy your achievements as well as your plans. Keep interested in your own career, however humble;

it is a real possession in the changing fortunes of time. Exercise caution in your business affairs, for the world is full of trickery. But let this not blind you to what virtue there is; many persons strive for high ideals, and everywhere life is full of heroism. Be yourself. Especially do not feign affection. Neither be cynical about love; for in the face of all aridity and disenchantment, it is as perennial as the grass. Take kindly the counsel of the years, gracefully surrendering the things of youth. Nurture strength of spirit to shield you in sudden misfortune. But do not distress yourself with dark imaginings. Many fears are born of fatigue and loneliness. Beyond a wholesome discipline, be gentle with yourself. You are a child of the universe no less than the trees and the stars; you have a right to be here. And whether or not it is clear to you, no doubt the universe is unfolding as it should. Therefore be at peace with God, whatever you conceive Him to be. And whatever your labors and aspirations, in the noisy confusion of life, keep peace in your soul. With all its sham, drudgery and broken dreams, it is still a beautiful world. Be cheerful. Strive to be happy.

PART TWO

# Looking the Part

# ·IX·

## Dressing for Your Role

WOMEN WHO WAIT for life to begin at forty haven't got much imagination. But a lot of women ought to shift gears around that time. Frenchmen maintain that a woman only begins to be interesting then—when she's found her identity. She has established her own style. She's poised and secure and she knows how to please a man.

If you haven't been brought up in Paris with a natural instinct for clothes, here are five rules of thumb to consider for starters:

1. Find your own style and have the courage to stick to it.

2. Choose your clothes for *your* way of life.

3. Make your wardrobe as versatile as an actress. It should be able to play many roles.

4. Find your happiest colors—the ones that make you *feel* good.

5. *Care* for your clothes, like the good friends they are!

Some women are walking around in the same styles that suited them when they were twenty. Oh, they go along with the current fashions to some extent—altering hemlines and adjusting shoulders—but their basic appearance doesn't undergo the changes that ought to be indicated by their maturity—which can be the loveliest time of their lives—or even by the era they're living in.

Sometimes women stick with the same "look" because it was the one their husbands fell in love with. Men are very strange. They'll fall for the first girl with a tight skirt and a sensational cleavage, and yet insist that their wives be very plain and modest. When you go out with your husband, see who he's talking to in a corner. Note what she's like. Attractive, of course. The first thing to do about that is to go and start talking to the most attractive *man* in the room—if possible, her husband!

But then, for heaven's sake, don't go home and start imitating that girl. Be more clever than that—be both the modest wife and the flirt. You *can* be both. The sexiest thing in the world isn't a see-through top, it's a garment that leaves something to the imagination. A flowing gown that covers a woman to the neck is much more seductive than a bikini.

But don't just rush out to buy the alluring gown and think that's all you need to attract his attention. You may have been Miss America of 1950—but do you *still* look like 1950? Does your husband see the same you every time he glances your way? Do you, in fact, see the same thing in your own mirror?

When a woman's whole fashion viewpoint needs an overhaul it's probably because she doesn't know her type. She might, a long time ago, have been a lithe outdoor tweedy girl who collected cashmere sweaters the way she collected beaux, wore a single strand of pearls, and combed her hair into a gleaming pageboy. She looked great. But has she still got a closet full of bulky tweeds in which she's no longer so lithe, and shelves of sweaters that reveal too much of her matronly bosom? But even if she regains her twenty-one-year-old figure, is she still the girl in the football stadium?

Knowing your type is probably one of the toughest things in the world. An actress has an advantage because there's a ruthless camera eye recording all the changes—and if she can't see them herself the director and a few hundred critics will. Other women just have to do their damnedest to be their own critics. One trick for finding your type is to study the styles worn by the world's best-dressed women. Most of them are over thirty-five, and many are over fifty. Those in the older brackets have found their own classic lines and made their intelligent adjustments to passing fashion.

They don't want to look like their daughters. They want their own very individual brand of chic. Their clothes are usually understated—certainly never flamboyant—and they pay more attention to detail than their daughters do. The cut and fit must be exactly right, and they're willing to spend hours in a fitting room to make sure of it. They spend money, too. But if any one of them went broke tomorrow she'd rather choose one perfectly cut expensive dress and make it do for years than buy a dozen cheap ones. These women plan to get at least two years out of a dress and three out of a coat, unless they are super-rich. As for suits, I know women wearing suits they bought ten years ago. Expensive suits, yes, but worth every penny in perennial elegance—the classic line again.

The intelligent woman adapts herself to fashion, but never to fad. She knows what is best for her, and her way of life, and sticks to it. She raises and lowers her hemline—with discretion—but she goes on with her timeless dresses made with the basic lines and fabrics that flatter *her*, define *her* life style. She's secure, and so she can be an elegant individual.


## A CANDID LOOK AT YOURSELF

A mirror usually doesn't get any message across because it's like a picture that's been hanging on the wall for as long as you can remember. You don't really see it any more. I think a marvelous stunt would be to have your best friend (or your most critical acquaintance) take some candid color snapshots of you from all angles, dressed just as you usually appear at, say, six in the evening. The same hair-do, the same makeup, and if possible the same expression on your face. Be honest! Be sure to have her take the rear views, too.

There ought to be some other shots of you wearing your best going-out-to-dinner dress, or your favorite bridge-with-the-girls costume—hat, gloves, bag, and costume jewelry. Everything. Then have that roll of film developed and *blown up*. You can't see much in a tiny snapshot. An eight-by-ten will show you the works—and you probably won't be very happy with it. Sit down and take a long look at that strange woman.

Is she today's with-it person—elegant, poised, groomed, glowing with health? Or is she a plump copy of Miss 1950? Is she sleek, or bumpy in the wrong places? How is her posture? Does she look better from the front than from the back? Does she stand gracefully? Knowing how to stand is a trick an actress should quickly learn. When I'm on my feet for hours at a reception I'm naturally more comfortable with them slightly apart. But the moment I give in to that temptation is the moment someone shoots a picture! Feet together, or one slightly in front of the other, is the most graceful stance. Look around at your next cocktail party and see how awkward many women look from the knees down.

The shock of taking a photographic inventory may send the average woman to bed for a week. But it could be the best thing that ever happened to her. I always pin my bad notices on my mirror. How about keeping those eight-by-ten candid shots around your dressing room for a while as you dress?

## GOOD TIMING IS GOOD FASHION

My own changes of style have run a tremendous gamut. In my early days in Hollywood I was so covered with ruffles, bows, and spangles that you could hardly notice *me*. And like Loretta Young, Connie Bennett, and all the others I plucked my eyebrows to a little line and drew a tiny little cupid's bow for a mouth. Off-screen, when I was dancing every night, my skirts were a little too short, my heels a little too high, and my hair a little too frizzy and a little too bright.

I wore brilliant red nail polish when everybody else wore pink, and when it was the thing to be fair I got a deep suntan. I loved being in the vanguard—and I was. They all followed along behind. This was the era when everybody wanted to be the complete flapper, to be noticed, to dance faster than anybody else.

I think my new look in makeup came when I made *Grand Hotel* with that wonderful cast, Greta Garbo, Wallace Beery, Lewis Stone, Jean Hersholt and both John and Lionel Barrymore, among others. I played the prostitute and I felt that a more sensuous look was needed. Full, natural lip line and generous eyebrows—no bra, no girdle. Definite features were called for, and I found that I liked that look so much I kept it.

It suited the kind of picture that was popular then, and the kind of femininity that was called for. Along with Garbo, Dietrich, Bankhead, Roz Russell, and Shearer I played languid *femmes fatales*. We had big, well-defined eyes, hollow cheeks, and generous mouths. We were temptresses. These, of course, were our film parts. In our private lives we were quite different.

For me the big switch came when Adrian started dressing me. Like Balenciaga he was always two years ahead of everyone else in fashion. He had a sense of timing that verged on genius. His timing was the kind that knew when a fashion had to change—and

*Overleaf: Two of the lovely dresses that Adrian designed for me—at left, from* The Bride Wore Red; *at right, from* Letty Lynton.

how. The importance of being *with* one's times. I was a flapper in the age of flappers. I became a sophisticated lady in the age of sophistication. (Though I certainly hope that if those eras had been reversed I wouldn't have tried to look like a flapper at the age of forty, any more than I want to look like a hippie now!)

Through Adrian's designs I often managed to promote fashions that spread like an epidemic. My films were some of his showpieces. He was the genius who created fashions that were in the best of taste. As almost everyone knows, he was the costume designer at Metro for many years and during the thirties and forties had a profound effect on the *haute couture.*

Adrian dressed only the top stars because that was all he had time for. Sometimes Shearer, Garbo, Roz Russell, and I were all working at one time, and he had to create costumes for each of our pictures, so there was no time left to dress the featured players. He made sketches, numbered them, and I'd stand and look at them and say, "Number One—Rich Girl, Number Three —Poor Girl," and so on.

Adrian understood the body and femininity and had a great sense of the right fabric and style for each of us. His cutting was perfection and he had an unerring sense of what was useful for a dramatic scene or what would distract from a dramatic scene. Most important, he knew all of us, and how we would play a scene—before we knew ourselves. He might cut a bodice very low and off center, as with one of my dresses in *Grand Hotel.* For a dramatic scene he always used black, or a dark color. And no distracting jewelry. In a comic scene, on the other hand, Adrian just let us go wild.

He also made great circular skirts for dancing, and lush, solidly beaded dresses, as well as chiffons—simple, elegant, feminine chiffons. No woman should be without one for a romantic evening. We introduced the tunic dress and, of course, the famous square-shouldered tailored ensemble with the very slim hip line that every woman loved and adopted.

I only wish I still had some of his clothes in my wardrobe today because his classic styles are coming back. When everyone was rushing back to Paris after the Second World War, he held the ground for American design. Not that he was the first American designer of *haute couture*. There was, and still is, the great Mainbocher. And there were Madame Frances and Hattie Carnegie, for whom Jean Louis designed, and, about the same time, Valentina—who did such fabulous things with jersey and made some of the most romantic evening gowns ever seen.

The first time Adrian saw me he uttered an unforgettable line: "You," he said, "are a female Johnny Weissmuller."

I just stood there. What could I do? Five feet, four and a half inches tall, with size twelve hips and size forty shoulders!

"Well, we can't cut 'em off," he said finally, "so we'll make them wider."

That was the start of a look that lasted for more than ten years. Broad padded shoulders, small waist, and slim hips. If a woman's hips weren't as slim as she would have liked, the shoulders made them seem so. I think that's one reason the style caught on so quickly. When I tried out for *Mildred Pierce* I showed up in a little cotton housedress that I'd bought off the rack at Sears— because that was the kind of thing Mildred would wear.

The director, Michael Curtiz, had a reputation for being "very difficult." It didn't take me long to find out *how* difficult. He took one look at me and snarled, "You and your damned shoulder pads!" reached out in fury, and ripped my dress from neck to hemline. Then he stared in shocked amazement. The shoulders were still there. They were real. I burst into tears and he strode off the set in total embarrassment. We got along pretty well after that.

163

Adrian always played down the designs for the big scene. For a lighter scene he'd create a "big" dress. His theory, of course, was that an absolutely stunning outfit would distract the viewer from the highly emotional thing that was going on. There should be just the actress, her face registering her emotions, the body moving to express her reactions—the dress is only background. But in the next scene, where she goes to the races and cheers for her horse, the costume must be absolutely smashing.

That trick shouldn't be reserved for the movies or the stage. I pass it on for any woman to use—and I think a great many women do use it, instinctively. For a romantic scene by candlelight, let your face and figure—and your expression—play the leading roles. Underdress. Play down the accessories. Leave the startling hat or jewel at home. For a public appearance, on the other hand, when I'm going to be mingling with hundreds of people, I try to give them something stunning to look at. I especially like to give them color.

## USE COLOR FOR YOUR SPIRITS

Basic black will never go out. But I think most women prefer happy black-and-white stripes, or red and white or blue and white. And gay prints. I revert to black when I'm traveling, particularly on a long trip, because it doesn't show the wrinkles so much. I get it in cotton. Cottons are so good now—preshrunk and with an attractive sheen—that they can look elegant even after a long flight.

A lot of women I know are afraid to wear hot pink because it takes a magnificent complexion. That's one shade that will show you up for what you really are. But it's stunning with a good suntan. I like lime green too. It looks so cool and is particularly lovely in linen—the light-weight linen that I live in.

(Heavy ones are fine when you put them on, but they do wrinkle and those wrinkles stay. You can't press them quickly, even with a steam iron. You have to wash out the whole dress.)

Although the right colors depend to some extent on the hair and eye colors, I think complexion is the most important consideration. A dress of the wrong shade can bring out sallowness, highlight blemishes, and add years to a woman's face. It will make her look hard. In general, mature women should avoid the bright, harsh shades—at least until they get to the grand dowager age of towering blue-white coiffures and royal purple. Muted shades, or pastels, in the colors that make a woman feel happiest are the safest ones to choose. Retiring too much into gray or beige isn't a good idea. But if you do buy a beige suit, be sure to brighten it with a scarf or a blouse that matches your eyes.

Color does so much for my spirits. Even in black-and-white films Adrian used to dress me in Wedgwood blue because it made me feel good. It gave me a happy feeling, even when the lines of the dress had to be severe for dramatic purposes.

## WHOM DO YOU DRESS FOR?

People are always debating whether we dress for men, for other women, or for ourselves. On occasion, I dress for all three. Femininity for men, color for women—and something very crazy, like a mad hat, for myself. But I don't know why there has to be a conflict. If you look good—if you're wearing what's *right for you,* and for the occasion—it will please everybody.

You may love a color your husband thinks he hates. For instance, the lady may adore turquoise—it matches her eyes. He saw her a long time ago in a turquoise dress and he said, "That color's just not for you, darling." Maybe it was the line of the dress that was wrong, or even the fabric. Or perhaps the occasion was an unhappy one. But whatever the cause, it's sunk deeply into his mind that he hates you in turquoise. So gently break him in with a pink dress with a little touch of turquoise at the throat —a scarf tucked in, not too much of it exposed, or a stunning turquoise necklace. He'll get a wonderful impression, and ten to one he'll say, "You're lovely in that dress!"—never knowing it's the scarf or the necklace that's turning on that pink and bringing something special out of your eyes. Next time you can go a little further, with a stole, say.

The fact is, most men are only conscious of an over-all look. If they claim they don't like green, or don't like velvet, perhaps it's a mistake that has nothing to do with the color or the fabric. Perhaps it mars the image that he wants of you—and that you should strive for. A man, without knowing a thing about fashion, can be a pretty good judge of whether a woman looks right. If he doesn't compliment you, find out why.

After you've taken a good look at those snapshots that you've had enlarged, take a good look at your wardrobe. Does it look as if it belongs to the woman in the pictures? Does it, in fact, look as if there's any coordination in it at all? Pick out the first dress that comes to hand. Okay, does it flatter your coloring— your hair, eyes, and complexion? Does the line do things for your figure that your figure isn't doing for itself? Or does it go against your figure? That's the worst thing in the world you can do. For instance, I can't wear Empire. It goes against my body line. My rib cage is too big. For that style you have to be flat-chested, and it gives you that beautiful long-legged look. On me—it looks as if I'm going to have quintuplets.

Does the dress in your hand spell out *your* personality, or is it trying to look like Raquel Welch or Mrs. Onassis, neither of whom happens to be your type?

If you honestly think the dress is right for you, where are you going to wear it? Does it fit into the kind of life you lead? (If you live in the country, what are you doing with all those town suits and hostess pajamas?) Supposing that dress is all right. If so, what shoes do you wear with it? What hat, gloves? Handbag, jewelry? Or is that lovely dress just hanging there without any accessories to keep it company? So many women fall in love with a dress, bring it home, and find absolutely nothing that will go with it. So it's left there alone in the dark. It's sad.

I feel as if clothes are people. When I buy a dress, or buy the fabric to have one made, that's a new friend. Am I to let it hang there and not give it warmth and affection? Course not! People love to do my clothes because I take such good care of them. I have a tremendous respect for fabrics.

## PLAN AND ACCESSORIZE

My rule: Don't buy a dress until you can afford all the right accessories and if, like me, you can't spend your life in hair curlers, have a hat made to match. I always get a yard and a half extra of the fabric I've ordered for a new dress. Half a yard for gloves and a yard for a turban or breton. Whatever state my hair is in I can still look well put together on a few minutes' notice.

I like matching coats for long dresses. They're a godsend on a summer evening when I'm not sure how steady the temperature is going to stay. And they have that wonderful planned look that says, see, I dressed with great care to come to your party! Every part of the costume is part of the whole effective picture.

If I have a suit made in a solid color I like a patterned silk blouse, and the jacket lined with the same fabric. If the skirt is lined, I use the patterned silk there, too. Probably nobody else will see the skirt lining, but knowing it's there makes me feel prettier, better dressed, and happier. It's wonderful what a couple of yards of material can do.

One of my fashion trademarks is to have even my shoes made to match my ensemble. Of course it would be folly to travel in silk shoes, so I have them covered in the same silk or fabric with transparent plastic over that, and they're always spotless. The dust comes off with a damp sponge.

## TAKE REGULAR INVENTORIES

Closets should be completely emptied twice a year. Four times a year is better. For one thing, there's probably a lot of dust in the corners that you haven't noticed, and a good airing won't do any harm. Then inspect every item in your wardrobe. Things you're doubtful about are probably all wrong. Maybe you're hanging on to them for some sentimental reason, or because you paid too much for them and hate to think you've wasted your money. But it's wasted already if the dress doesn't flatter you, so be brave and get rid of it. Give things away to someone they do compliment, or send them to a charity or a thrift shop and resolve not to make the same mistakes again.

That old saw, "When in doubt, don't," is never so true as when it comes to clothes. Or getting married.

I know some terribly rich ladies who do something I can't afford. They rent a whole room in a storage warehouse and twice a year send down their clothes (on hangers and covered in plastic) to be kept for the following season. If they happen to need an out-of-season costume for a trip they can go in and pick out a few things. Otherwise they know that their clothes are being kept at perfectly controlled temperatures. Everything, of course, is cleaned before it goes into storage, and since we're never sure what the hemlines will be in four or five months I have one friend who stores her dresses with the hems let out.

People with big houses can sometimes have such storage rooms built in the basement or the attic. But it's important that there are no extremes of temperature and that the rooms can be completely sealed against dust and dampness.

During these seasonal inventories, use your full-length mirror, and use it in a good light. There's no excuse for not having a good mirror even if you must give up some little luxury in order to buy one. Better still, have a triple mirror—the kind you find in dress-shop fitting rooms—that enables you to see yourself coming and going. That "going" look may give you something to ponder over. Some women never have the faintest idea how they look from behind, and yet people see them from that angle half the time!

I used to say to my twins, "You know, you kids look as if you'd made up and dressed in some dark closet." Their makeup would be sloppy, their slips showing, and the scarf wouldn't go with the sweater. But they were growing up and making the usual mistakes. No adult woman should ever look as if she dressed in a dark closet.

## START FROM SCRATCH

You may be lucky if your inventory cleans out the closet so you have to start all over again from scratch. It could be the best thing that ever happened to your fashion image and your morale. (I'm not so sure about your husband's morale.) If this happens, study the fashion magazines, talk to friends, and see if you can find a knowledgeable and interested saleswoman. Try on a lot of things and take plenty of time analyzing each one for all the important points. If a dress passes the first exam, ask yourself where it's going to go with you, and how often. There's no point in buying a ball gown first if you go to only one ball a year. And maybe last year's cocktail dresses will do while you get some of the right things to wear for a busy life during the day.

When you're ready to say yes to the purchase, go out into the shop and take up a position about twenty feet from a full-length mirror. Walk toward yourself. Do you like what you see coming? Is it a lot better than the image you saw when you first walked into the store? If so, wrap it up, pay for it—but don't go home until you're sure you have exactly the right accessories. You should be ready to emerge in your new ensemble the next day, because you should never have to alter more than a hemline. If there's any other place where the fit isn't right, leave the dress in the store, unless you're a good seamstress yourself.

By this time you have discovered you have a "look" that is unique. It's entirely your own, and you should stick to it. As I said before, this is what the best-dressed women do. Edith Head, the designer, has what she calls her "uniform." She designed the first shell—the loose blouse and skirt and the casual, easy-fitting cardigan jacket. She has them in every known color and fabric but usually the same style because she knows what's good for her, and she sticks to it. She says, "Don't be a fashion sheep. Be a fashion fence-sitter. There is a norm in every season. There is always normalcy in the background. Select what is right for *you.*"

Florence Walsh, my New York secretary, has what her family calls her uniform. She wears her own thing better than anybody I know. Never *fussy*, but in perfect taste, and just right for her. She doesn't like sheer silks or clinging things. For a party she will change, perhaps, into a lovely turquoise dress in a softer fabric. But it's still simple, and still uniquely Florence.

It's a big problem when a dress receives too many compliments.

Then you want to wear it constantly. As a result it rarely goes to the cleaners and begins to look tired before its time. If a dress is that much of a success have it copied or buy it in another fabric, another color. Losing a favorite dress for a week to a dry cleaner can be a hardship. In the picture business and in TV we have a cleaner called Malone, whose staff picks up the wardrobe we've been wearing during the day around seven-thirty or eight in the evening and have it back at five the next morning. I use a place in New York, Altman Cleaners, that's almost as wonderful. I can send things out one day and have them back the next afternoon.

## DRESS TO DISGUISE FIGURE FAULTS

It's a rare woman who has exactly the proportions she wants, even with exercise and diet. Most of us are born with bones that are short where they should be long and wide where we'd like them narrow. Learn to camouflage the points you don't like.

A woman with a short neck, for instance, should never wear turtlenecks. She'll look like a turtle. Nor big, chunky necklaces or up-tight scarves. Her necklines should be set out on her shoulders and a V-line will give an illusion of length. She should wear short hair, and button earrings instead of dangling ones. A woman with too long a neck can just reverse all those directions and get a beautiful effect.

A woman I know is very high-waisted. She can never wear belts. They look as if they're hanging around her neck. So she never defines her waist. Her hips are narrow and she looks well in tunics, longer jackets, and blouses that come down over the top of the skirt, Cossack-style.

Broad hips aren't hidden by a dirndl or a full skirt. It only exaggerates them. The best trick to draw the eye away from width

*171*

is to dress with vertical lines. Skirts shouldn't be cut on the bias below the waist. Candy stripes are flattering.

On the other hand, a tall slim woman can bring herself into better proportion by using horizontal lines, bias cuts, and large prints with stunning cinched-in belts.

Pants are probably here to stay. But they shouldn't stay long on any but the most lithe and slim-hipped. I love Pucci pants for Capri, Jamaica, or Barbados. I live in them in the Islands. Everyone there does. You only need a cocktail dress if you go to Government House. But I don't see them, for me at least, on a city street or in a restaurant. Even the new dressy pants suits—they are for home.

I'm now getting up the courage to have an evening dress made with a slit up the side, to the thigh. I've always had a little slit to just above the knee because I've been wearing my skirts just below the knee—throughout all the mini period—and with a straight skirt I need that little slit to walk. I think the long slit on an evening gown gives the body such a lovely kind of movement. It *suggests* sex, but not overtly, in the same way that a piece of chiffon between two bodies is far more sexy than just skin.

## JEWELRY

Jewelry is an essential accessory. I would feel undressed without my costume jewelry. I never travel with good things any more. It seems a pity. You work all your life to be able to afford good things and then you have to keep them in a vault at the bank. But such beautiful costume jewelry is made now that most of the wealthiest women in the world leave their precious jewels in the safe and confidently wear the imitations.

Brian Bishop designs most of my costume jewelry. He says that I do more than half the job, but I guess we just work well to-

*This is costume jewelry—a bib necklace of orange and jade-green stones set in gold, with earrings to match.*

*Above, a versatile diamond necklace. The pendant at the bottom can be worn as a brooch or broken into two clips. The earrings match. At left, a necklace of freshwater pearls and diamonds with matching earrings— which are always in the vault!*

175

gether. I choose a color I need, he studies the fabric of a new dress, and he creates ingenious matching sets. It's important that jewelry match. A turquoise necklace with amethyst earrings is a crime. It's like wearing rubber boots with a chiffon skirt. Brian makes me extensions—a necklace that, with another link, becomes a hip-line belt. We hold one philosphy in common which was expounded by the great Valentina: When you finish a creation, take something off. Diminish, diminish, diminish. It's the woman herself who's important.

Brian's costume jewelry is not in the five-and-ten-cent-store category, but I do have some things that are really inexpensive. Recently I bought a pair of earrings for two dollars that are absolutely lovely—big gypsy loops that fit close to my face and neck.

Earrings do wonderful things for the eyes. It takes time for a man to notice what's on your hands or wrists, but the first time he looks at you he sees your face, and your earrings spark up your eyes and say, Aren't I pretty! They're especially a must for me because I often wear my hair back, or upswept, and without them I look unfinished.

## HATS

Walter Florell used to make my hats. He'd come to me with reams of hatboxes full of lovely creations to be tried on. But he had some inflexible rules. One day he said, "Miss Crawford, I've been coming to you when you've been in full makeup—that is, street makeup—and I know it's eight o'clock in the morning. I'm not going to ask you to put on full makeup, but please put on lipstick—and earrings."

I said, "But, Walter, if I think I look good in the hat without the lipstick and the earrings, I know damn well that I'll look better and greater with them on."

He shook his head. "I have a strict rule for anyone trying on my hats." And he was right. When you try on a new hat, look your best, wear street makeup, and wear earrings.

Hats aren't seen around as much as they used to be. There are some prominent hat makers who, in a panic, have started to manufacture wigs. I don't often use wigs except when I'm making a picture, and I can't wash my hair every day except when I'm shooting. So I travel with wigs and three-quarter falls. I comb my own front hair up over the falls and twist my own hair under in back. I use a French twist and count on beautiful hats to make me look as if I've just come out of a beauty salon. Only my hairline shows under my hat. I don't like hair around my face. It just isn't right for me. Even when my hair is perfectly set, a hat adds still more. It frames the face. It's feminine and provocative. To me, a well-dressed woman without a hat is like an oil painting without a frame around it.

## FRAGRANCE IS FEMININE

Your final accessory is perfume. I always wear colognes during the day. I can't get around to perfume before four o'clock in the afternoon. Perfumes are overpowering to the people you work with, and a little too much for daytime, I think. But a whiff of the right cologne—the right one for a woman's particular personality—should be served right up with the bacon and eggs.

I love the spicy fragrances and I used to wear Jungle Gardenia but it got too heavy for me. The same scent doesn't suit a woman all her life or, in fact, for every occasion.

177

French women choose a scent when they're girls and use it until they're grandmothers. It becomes their trademark.

"Ah," he murmurs in the dark theater, "Giselle is here tonight!"

But *I* think that a woman usually outgrows a fragrance every decade or so. There are just three that I would never want to live without: Estée Lauder's *Youth Dew* spray cologne, Lanvin's *Spanish Geranium,* and *Royall Lyme,* a man's cologne. I shall be faithful to them.

## CARING FOR YOUR WARDROBE

A wardrobe needs its right home. I'm very fortunate. I've been able to have many extra cupboards and shelves built into my apartment with ample room for everything. Well, not quite ample, but I manage. Because I travel so much in different climates, and because I make so many public appearances, I have to have more changes than most women. It's part of my job and, to some extent, my clothes are *my* uniform. But on a smaller scale any woman should plan the right accommodations for her clothes.

My dresses always go into their individual plastic bags, pinned to canvas-covered wooden hangers in a special way so that they'll hang right. (Some hangers do terrible things to the shoulder line.) Matching gloves are pinned to the hanger with each dress.

For shoes and handbags, I have a small room with shelves, floor to ceiling, lining the three walls. My shoes are always put away with trees in them—and if I run out of trees I stuff them with tissue paper. I sandwich them together, fasten them with an elastic band, and slip them into a plastic bag. On top, or under-

*Not the kind of hat I usually wear! It's a replica of Maurice Chevalier's famous straw hat.*

neath, is the matching handbag in its own plastic bag. Oversized handbags go on a deeper shelf, and boots have their own deep shelf on top.

My dressing room has a whole wall of boxlike compartments designed to hold my hats, many of which are fragile, and none of which should ever be crushed. I stuff them with tissue paper and group them by color so that I can quickly put my hand on the hot pink, the orange, or whatever was made to match my dress. I have the usual size shelves for sweaters and scarves.

My most important rule is: *Never put anything back soiled.* Things get hung up at night, but first thing in the morning I bring them out in daylight to see if there's a water spot, a grease spot, a smudge. If there is, Mamacita takes the dress away and sees that it doesn't go back into the closet until it's been to the cleaners—pristine, pressed, and ready to wear again. This not only saves time and bother, it saves the clothes. Nothing ruins them so quickly as being left dirty and wrinkled until you find time to care for them and if you wait, it's a big job. This way, it's a matter of minutes each morning.

Necklines usually need attention. A high neck just can't help getting powder smudges. For washables Mamacita lays the collar on the counter in the kitchen and uses a special spot cleaner along the soiled area. She lets it sit for ten minutes and then plunges the whole garment into cold water with cold-water liquid soap.

I'm lucky to be able to have my clothes made to my own sketches. Sometimes I envy women who can walk into a store, pick something off the rack, and say, "I'll take it!" I've never been able to do that. Forty bust, ten waist, and twelve hips are my sizes, reading from top to bottom. If I walk into a store and ask for a size forty (for my shoulders) they say, "Don't be ridiculous. We don't go beyond fourteen." I went into Saks a few days ago and saw some beautiful things—dress-and-coat ensembles. I tried on a size eighteen and couldn't move my arms.

When I stop at a house like Dior or Givenchy they'll say, "Yes, Miss Crawford. It's a size six, isn't it? Or an eight?"

When I ask them, "What's the largest size you have already made up?" The answer will be—a ten. I can never wait to have such houses make anything for me in Paris because the fitting rooms are booked so far in advance and they require so many fittings. Besides, at their prices I'd have to be a millionaire, which I'm not.

So I make my sketches, select my fabrics from Corroyer, and send them to three Japanese girls in Hollywood, Fumi, Jenny, and Lilly. They have my form there and I don't dare gain half an inch or the clothes they send back won't fit me.

My shoes and handbags are made by André, in New York, and my hats by Emme and Vincent and Bill. Gloves are made by Mrs. Levine. I wear high heels because I'm only five feet four and a half and I like to be visible in a crowd. They're so much more flattering to the feet, ankles, and legs too. In hats, my perennial favorites are turbans and bretons. I have a great many straw hats—small bretons with wide brims, and some way-up-high bretons with brims coming above the crown. They never go out of style because they're so flattering. I like sailors, too. In fact, as is pretty well known, I like hats!

At the start, I laid down five rules for dressing well. Here are a few afterthoughts:

*Understate*—or as Valentina said, "diminish." Let your face be more important than your costume.

If you think you may be wearing too much jewelry, you are.

Ask your husband how he thinks you look. If he says, "That's a lovely dress," try again. What he should say is, "*You* look lovely!"

# ·X·

# A Program for a Lovely Figure

Years ago there was a Helen Hokinson cartoon in *The New Yorker* of an overpadded matron regarding herself sorrowfully in the mirror of a dress shop.

"But it looked so lovely in the window," she was saying.

It really was a pathetic drawing, and it probably rang bells with millions of women. The most beautiful clothes look awful draped over a shapeless form. And, conversely, a really good figure can wear a twenty-dollar dress with verve.

## HOW TO STAND AND WALK

Most figure faults are fairly minor, if you watch yourself. They involve dropping a few pounds, losing a couple of inches here and there, and getting firmed up. Above all, a good carriage can correct half a dozen so-called faults in seconds. People have always thought that I was a tall woman. Because I try to walk tall. When I move I pull myself up as if I'm being manipulated on wires. It's second nature now, but it certainly stems from the fact that I was a dancer.

Have you ever noticed how lovely ballet dancers always look, even when they're walking down the street or across a living room? They not only carry themselves like angels, they have happy expressions because for years they work all day in front of mirrors. And you can't keep looking into a mirror at a disagreeable expression. A busy woman can't spend whole days in front of mirrors, but she ought to have them all over the house (which improves the décor, too) and make a point of glancing at herself every time she passes one. It's a form of narcissism that pays off. If *you* are pleased with what you see, chances are he will be, too.

It's commonplace to find people who look old at forty, or young at sixty. The reason isn't the number of little wrinkles that may be sprouting, but in the way they use their bodies. "Old" people have lost their flexibility. Their joints stiffen up from lack of use. Their capillaries constrict and less blood comes through to the tissues. That means the complexion is undernourished, too. And everything starts to taper off. When they stop moving vigorously they slow down mentally. They're old in their minds even when they're still on the happy side of middle age. And it shows!

On the other hand, look at Lynn Fontanne, Helen Hayes, Katharine Hepburn—who did such a fantastic dance in *Coco* and who plays an almost professional game of tennis—and Margot Fonteyn, who still dances like a dream. Those ladies will never be old. And Cary Grant is still as much adored by teenagers as he was decades ago. They all have at least one thing in common. They move with the most perfect grace, almost as if they're two inches above the ground. And they stand up as if they're proud of themselves—and they damn well should be!

As for mental youthfulness, Goethe and Michelangelo did their best work in their eighties. (Covering the ceiling of the Sistine Chapel can be pretty good exercise.) And consider Picasso, Casals, Sir Winston Churchill, and Grandma Moses!

The only time I ever had to stop moving around was when I was sixteen years old. I was described by the man who hired me for my first Broadway job as "the little fat girl with blue eyes." I weighed 145 pounds, but it wasn't fat. It was sheer hard muscle from dancing. I couldn't begin to take off weight until I'd *melted* those muscles. I had to stay practically immobile until they disappeared and I could reshape myself. I was very stupid then in the way I dieted. I lived on crackers and mustard and black coffee. Luckily I was young and healthy. I survived.

My favorite sports, swimming and tennis, are *stretch* sports. I especially like swimming in the sea because salt water is my best medicine. One year when I had a terrible cold that threatened to ruin my whole winter I went down to Jamaica, soaked up sun and salt water, and was completely cured in two days. I once got caught in a bad undertow at Atlantic City and got a permanent scare, so now I swim long distances parallel to the shore. Drowning isn't the way I want to go.

Both swimming and dancing strengthened my chest and back muscles, so that I'm often able to go without a bra—even in films. One day when I was sick my stand-in tried to replace me in a long shot. The producer and the cameraman said it wouldn't work, because she wore a bra in that scene and I didn't. Some bets were made, and they won, because of course they could see her bra line in back.

I sit on hard chairs—soft ones spread the hips. Unlike Oscar Levant, who said he never stood when he could sit and never sat when he could lie down, I stand and walk as much as I can. I don't think any of us walk enough, especially those of us who have desk work to do. When the work is done, the day is gone, and we take the shortest (sitting-down) route home. A walk before bedtime is the best cure for insomnia as well as a way of getting a little more exercise.

Once when I was in Paris I spoke to a doctor about some difficulty I had in getting to sleep. I wanted some pills.

He said, "Buy a big red apple. Eat half of it at the Place de la

Concorde and the other half at the Étoile. That's my prescription." Meaning, of course, that I'd get in a nice two-mile walk before bed.

Too bad one can't walk in New York City alone at night. And it's so sad to think that none of us can walk in Central Park at night any more; if it were safe, I'd do it. It's a prescription I believe in.

A beautiful woman stands beautifully. In the first place, she doesn't jitter, she doesn't keep swaying from one foot to the other, and she doesn't constantly use her hands. Girls who wear their hair over their faces use their ears as hangers, pushing it back behind their ears—making such a commotion that people don't know what the hell they're talking about, let alone what they look like. Tugging at your dress or fiddling with your belt is just as distracting. If your dress doesn't fit, leave it at home. Throw it away, or learn how to sew.

People often mistake movement for activity, for vivaciousness. As an actress I learned to use my hands very little. I used to rehearse with my hands tied behind my back so that I'd never fall into the habit of using them constantly.

Stand serenely, then. And stand tall. My little trick for holding myself straight is to imagine that a wire is attached to the middle of my chest bone, pulling it *up*, not out. Somehow, then, everything else falls into the right alignment.

High heels help. I like to rehearse my big scenes in bare feet. I always feel that I'm drawing strength right out of the ground. But when I was doing *The Virginian* and it came time to shoot, the director, Robert Gist, would say, "Put on your high heels."

"But then I'll be too tall for Sara Lane," I'd say.

"So we'll put the rest of the cast on a box. But I want *you* in heels. Because those heels will act like a ramrod through your backbone."

## A Program for a Lovely Figure

He was right. Women have been wearing low heels for several years now, and I admit they're comfortable, but the ladies I've observed have been slouching more than they used to.

Beautiful carriage means that a straight line can be drawn from the inside of your foot, through the center of your thigh, the center of your pelvis, the center of your shoulders, and the crown of your head. Stand with your back to the wall. Heels against the wall, then calves, then buttocks. Lead with pelvis. Then shoulders. Then reach for the ceiling with the top of your head. Beautiful movement means that your legs move freely from the hips, not from the knees. It means a confident stride with the arms swinging naturally and the top of your head—not your chin—just a little bit elevated.

I advise girls to "look to the stars." I don't mean that in a philosophical sense—although that could certainly apply. I mean that a lifted head insures a lovely neckline—and, confidence.


At times I've deliberately gained weight. I did for *Mildred Pierce* because I thought it suited the part. Sometimes I gain a little while I'm making a picture because with all that hard work I need more energy. But the best condition I was ever in was when I was doing *What Ever Happened to Baby Jane?* in a wheel chair. I had to wheel myself around, push myself back and forth, turn quickly, and I was the thinnest I've been in years. I weighed only 119 pounds. And firm and hard as a brickbat. (Get a wheel chair and try doing your housework in it!) Part of that strenuous role was learning how to get myself in and out of bed, from and into the wheel chair. I learned how from a young paraplegic, a Korean air ace who was injured in a crop-duster plane crash *after* he got safely back home from the war. He taught me how to hoist my body into the bed first and then lift each leg. And how to fall out of the chair—straight forward, and then roll over. I practiced over and over with that wheel chair at home, on weekends.

This isn't one of my favorite formulas for getting in good shape, but if you should ever get a broken leg it could be the silver lining to *that* cloud! The day the cast is off you'll leap up sleek as a seal.

At any rate, for a body that gets you around at a good healthy pace and carries clothes beautifully, a woman (or a man) has to combine regular exercise with the right diet. There is no magic solution. And there are *no* pills that will do anything but make you sick.

## SPORTS AND GADGETS

For just keeping fit generally, nothing beats sports—outdoors and with your husband. Sports have always been part of my life and because of them I haven't had to have too many of those boring sessions down on the floor. Play tennis or squash and don't call it exercise, call it fun.

There are many sports that can be taken up in "middle age"— an expression I hate. But anyway, you're not eighteen any more, and it's too late to try out for the hundred-yard dash. But it's never too late for skiing—both snow and water. Or for golf. Swinging a club doesn't take too much energy, and you get a nice brisk walk.

I have friends who say bowling is a good thing. And nothing can beat mountain climbing. A couple might combine it with hunting, bird watching, or the study of flowers. Or just climb the damned mountain because it's there. It really doesn't matter so long as you're both out there, moving vigorously through clean air, and together.

A Program for a Lovely Figure

As I write this, jogging is the thing to do. (Prize fighters have been doing it for centuries.) There's a gadget on the market about the size of a bath mat, slightly slanted, called the Executive Jogger. If you prance up and down on it for three minutes twice a day it's supposed to be the equivalent of jogging for two miles uphill.

I'm in favor of any gadget that gets people moving. If they can't get out and jog two miles in the fresh air (in a city like New York that isn't easy), then I'm for opening wide the windows, pollution and all, and jogging for a few minutes on this little device.

If there's room in your house for an exercycle I approve of that, too. If there's a basement, why not a rowing machine? The whole family could go down there for nightly workouts before dinner and feel much better for it. In my city apartment I have no houseroom for things like that, but I do have a hard-rubber stretcher that gives my muscles a workout I love.

I don't knock any gadget that comes along—as long as it encourages people to keep flexible.

S-T-R-E-T-C-H

When I can't get to sea water or to a tennis court, or out for a long, brisk walk, I work on stretch exercises at home. One that I do many times a day as I move around my apartment involves standing for a moment with my back against a wall. I dig my heels into the floor, stand straight, and place the palm of my hand between the small of my back and the wall. Keeping my chin level, I pull the crown of my head toward the ceiling. At the same time I push the small of my back toward the wall until there's no longer room for my hand.

Someone watching me do this one day said that I actually appeared to grow two inches in a few seconds.

## THE SLANT BOARD

I *should* put in fifteen minutes twice a day on my slant board. Like most women I tell myself that I'm too busy, but I know I could get up a little earlier, or find a quarter of an hour before I dress for dinner. Or, when my secretary leaves, I lie there returning my phone calls. I lie there for fifteen minutes stretching . . . stretching . . . trying to reach the wall behind me with the top of my head. *Not* with the chin, because that pulls the neck in the wrong way. Then, when I feel all long, lithe, and limber, I get down to my other exercises on a hard floor. I prefer that to exercising on the slant board because I get so energetic that I roll off. Slant boards should be made much, much wider.

There are a number of effective exercises for special problems that I'll describe farther on. But if I'm not bulging in any particular place I like to get my regular workouts while I'm working or doing other things. I'll describe a few of these.

## WHILE-DOING-SOMETHING-ELSE EXERCISES

Whenever I have to pick something off the floor I bend down, keeping my legs straight. Dutifully touching your toes fifty times every day is a crashing bore. But there are almost as many times when something has to be picked up anyhow—or a lower drawer has to be opened—so I automatically do it in a manner that keeps me fit. I try to make a graceful stretching gesture out of reaching for things on high shelves, too. I don't make it easier by dragging out a little step stool.

While I'm on the phone I take a small bottle—a Pepsi bottle, of course—and roll it back and forth under my instep. I touch first the heel to the floor, then the toe, ten times for each foot. (This is just about long enough to phone in my grocery order.) These exercises strengthen the foot, stretch the calf muscles, and result in lovely feet and legs.

When I'm standing—scraping carrots, or just waiting somewhere—I dig my heels into the ground, draw myself up to my best posture, and pull my stomach muscles in *hard*.

I like the isometrics that can be done while I'm busy at something else. When I'm dictating to my secretary I may raise my elbows level with my shoulders and press the heels of my hands hard against each other. (The whole idea behind isometrics is to make the muscles work against each other.) This exercise, lasting for just six to ten seconds, is wonderful for the inside of the upper arms—the place that can go flabby almost overnight and make it impossible to wear sleeveless dresses.

For the backs of the upper arms, do the same exercise with the hands raised just above the level of the forehead.

The two combined take less than a minute. Do them several times a day. Even when you're watching your favorite TV show you don't have to slouch back with your feet up, and cultivate rounded shoulders, curvature of the spine, and a protruding belly. You can get your shoulders back where God meant them to be while you're watching a lovely young actress who moves like an angel.

Sit up in your chair (or sit cross-legged, Yogi-style, on the floor) and put your hands behind you. Grasp one wrist with the other hand and *press* both hands into the small of your back as if you were trying to push right through to the front. Push hard—and just hold it for three seconds (during the first commercial). Round shoulders are an old-lady look, and they can pretty quickly develop into that awful thing called a dowager's hump. This is one exercise you can't get enough of—and luckily there are plenty of commercials.

## DON'T JUST STAND THERE

You're on your feet. Maybe you're phoning, or combing your hair, or taking off your makeup. Plant your bare feet about twelve inches apart and grip the floor with them, keeping your knees rigid. Then try to push your feet together—but without letting them budge. Try as hard as you can. This is a wonderful example of getting muscles to work against each other and it's a tremendous thing for the inner thighs—they are another terribly flab-prone area. If they're not taunt and smooth you can forget about getting out on the beach or around the swimming pool. This exercise can, and should, be done a dozen times a day—while you're making the stew or waiting for a bus. (No, it's not noticeable to people passing by.) Or skimming through the morning paper. A newspaper doesn't have to be read sitting down! And don't wait until the inner thighs have begun to sag—this should be a *preventive* routine.

## REAL PROBLEMS

All the movements I've mentioned can be done casually during the course of an ordinary busy day, while you're doing something else. But for real problems—and who hasn't one or two?—you just have to make time for organized work.

*A Program for a Lovely Figure*

*Hips:* Lucky is the woman who doesn't, from time to time, have to deal with hips that are an inch or two bigger than they should be.

One of my favorite routines for keeping my rear in good form is to sit down on the floor and "walk" across it on my buttocks, holding my arms out straight in front for balance, and then "walk" back again, backwards. It's good for the abdomen, too, because of course you have to keep your legs raised and straight out. And to keep your balance you have to keep your back straight —which helps your posture. Two or three of these fanny walks a day, depending on the size of your room, are a very good three-in-one improvement program.

For more hip improvement—and the waist, too—I lie on my back with my elbows on the floor at my sides. With my legs straight out I make my knees touch the floor on either side, *keeping my shoulders and elbows firmly on the floor.*

Then I stretch my arms out to the sides, I raise my knees as far as I can and bring them over my left shoulder to my left elbow, and then back and over to touch my right elbow. No fair elbow lifting to help it along! When you've succeeded in touching your elbows with your knees, then try to touch the floor. This does wonderful things for your waist, too.

*Firming Stomach Muscles:* Lie on your back with arms straight out at your sides and *very slowly*, with knees straight, raise your legs high and hold them in the air. Take a deep breath and *very slowly* lower them again.

Then, with your legs still against the floor, draw the small of your back into the floor until you can feel that your back is one straight line. Hold for a count of ten.

Then begin the leg-raising exercise again. Work up to ten times.

As your stomach muscles become firmer add this routine:

Anchor your feet under the bed or a heavy armchair and raise and lower your body slowly, keeping your knees rigid and your back very straight.

The muscles in the abdomen are a woman's weakest and they deserve all the attention she can give them if she wants a lovely figure. Even skinny girls often have protruding stomachs if they don't have good muscle tone.

## MOST MEN ARE LEG WATCHERS

I've mentioned some exercises that can tone up good legs that have been neglected. But some legs seem to be the wrong shape to begin with. A certain amount of recontouring *can* be achieved.

Have you ever been in Holland and wondered why all the women have large calves? They weren't born with them. They start riding bicycles as soon as they can toddle and go on cycling into their dotage. Great exercise, but too much of it produces what used to be called ballet-dancer legs.

If calves are too large because they're solid muscle, the best answer I know is the way I lost weight when I was sixteen—immobilizing myself until the muscle melted. At the same time you should follow a sensible diet designed to lose pounds all over. There are claims that certain diets will get weight off here, others will shed inches off there. But it just isn't so. Cut down calorie intake and inches will slough off nicely everywhere.

*For curvier calves, or slimmer ones:*

1. Whenever you walk through a doorway at home, stop, press the palms of your hands flat against the top of the door frame, get up on your toes, then push up with your arms and try to get your heels back on the floor. *But don't let them budge*—you're pushing

against the calf muscles and recontouring them. Hold it for a few seconds and then go on about your chores.

2. Sit on a straight chair, point your toes out straight, and kick up as high as you can with each leg. You'll feel a healthy pull in the calf muscles.

3. After a few of the kicks, stand up on your toes and lower yourself very slowly to a squatting position, still keeping your weight on the balls of your feet. Then pull slowly up again. It's fair to balance yourself lightly with your hands on the back of a chair if you have to.

4. Put a book on the floor and place the balls of your feet on the book and your heels on the floor. Raise yourself slowly until you're on tiptoe on the book. Then lower yourself just as slowly. The thicker the book, the better the results.

These four exercises will slim down fat calves and build up thin ones. The point is that the muscles are being firmed, and no matter what your problem the result is lovelier legs.

*Ankles, too:* I've described one of my favorites for keeping the ankles slim—rolling a Pepsi bottle under the arch of the foot. Another simple exercise is to stick your leg out straight and, not moving it, rotate your foot in wide circles in both directions for a minute or two. Then push your foot up and down for a couple of minutes more.

Just dancing will accomplish ankle and calf recontouring. If you don't go dancing every night, put on some records and find ways of dancing through your housework. Shoving a vacuum cleaner or a mop might turn out to be fun if you invent some imaginative ballet steps to do around the room at the same time. The music will help to keep you going. An LP lasts for about twenty minutes—a good way to time your housecleaning *and* the time you spend on lovely legs.

*Thighs:* If your thighs are a special problem you will have to get down on the floor again. Here are seven exercises to firm all the muscles in that area:

1. Lie on your side with one arm stretched out under your head. Bring the knee of the upper leg slowly up to your chest, and slowly back into position again. Do this a few times (to dreamy music) and then roll over and do it with the other leg.

2. In the same position on your side, raise the upper leg and move it forward and back as far as you comfortably can. Roll over and do this with the other leg.

3. Raise the top leg and raise the bottom leg up to meet it. Slowly lower the bottom leg, and then the top one.

These three exercises, all done from the same starting position, are good for the buttocks as well as the outside of the thighs. They should be done as often as possible, on both sides, and as long as possible for the quickest results. If you like wearing slim skirts, there's nothing uglier than having two additional bulges just below where the hips naturally curve. And of course if you have them you can't possibly wear pants.

4. For the inside of the thighs, lie on your back with your knees up, feet flat on the floor, and put a small rubber ball between your knees. Squeeze the ball, and hold it with all the muscle pressure you can.

5. Kneel, with your knees apart, and try to bring the knees together. But don't let them move. Pull until you feel the tug on the inside thigh muscles and hold it as long as you comfortably can—or a little longer.

6. Now sit on the floor, and press the soles of your feet together. Press your knees down, to either side, as far as you can. Keep pressing till it hurts. (But don't cheat and push with your hands!)

7. The simple old ballet warm-up of kicking will wake up the thigh muscles all around. Put one hand on a sturdy chair or

railing and, *holding yourself absolutely erect* and keeping both legs straight, kick forward as high as you can, several times. Then kick out to the side, making sure your body is straight as a ramrod. Then kick straight back. Do the same thing with the other leg.

You may not get very high kicks the first day or two, but you'll be surprised at the way you can gain an inch in altitude each time until you're making a pretty good showing. And your legs will be looking prettier every day. If you can manage this in front of a mirror, as ballet dancers do, you can keep better track of your carriage, and your progress.

## LEGS IN GENERAL

There are two more things that I do regularly to keep my legs the way I want them:

1. I just walk around my apartment with my toes pointed straight in. Of course one looks like a pigeon, so do it when you're alone. But try always to walk that way when you're puttering around alone. You'll feel all the leg muscles responding.

2. Bend down and put your palms flat on the floor, keeping your knees straight. Then walk "four-legged" across the room (or down the hall if you're sure you won't frighten anyone) and backwards again. This is wonderful for both arm and leg muscles, and it draws blood to the face, which helps the complexion.

## START SLOWLY AND DON'T BE DISCOURAGED

On-the-floor exercises are only safe (and comfortable) if you do them on a mat, or on several layers of Turkish towels. Don't wear constricting underwear. Use a leotard, or nothing at all. After all, you're in the privacy of your room.

Always warm up to exercising. You can't suddenly jolt a stiff body into a rigorous workout. My doctor has told me that the best time to exercise is at the end of the day, before dinner, when the body is limber and a little fatigued. Begin slowly by swinging your arms around in a circle. Do a little jogging in place. Get your circulation going to fuel your muscles.

Do your exercises to music. It will cheer you up and the rhythm will keep you at a regular pace. As your body gets used to all this unexpected activity you can do each exercise just about as often and as long as you like. But start gently.

I know that the trouble with some of the more strenuous movements is that when you first try them, if you haven't moved around in a long time, you find yourself so far from the goal. It's an awful temptation to say, "Well, I guess it's too late for me to try this one. I'll never make it. I'm twelve inches from where I should be!" But it's amazing how, after a short time, most people *do* succeed in reaching their goal.

Muscles are remarkably cooperative things. If you give them half a chance they'll respond, they're so damned grateful that they're being used again. I'd say, never give up in less than two weeks of conscientious trying. Or a month! The trying will stimulate the circulation, and as a good supply of blood reaches all the muscles and sinews it's like oiling a machine that's been neglected. It will start to run again. It may just amaze you.

It's certainly better to have been moving vigorously all your life, as I have, but it's never too late to get moving again. I know a man who started this kind of regime after his seventieth birthday. I doubt if he'd been doing much more than moving from his desk to his car for decades. But after a short time he was able to do every one of the exercises I've mentioned, and several more. And says he feels twenty years younger. So it really can be done!

## KEEP APPOINTMENTS WITH YOUR FIGURE

For serious problems you should schedule two sessions a day: half an hour before lunch and half an hour before dinner. Write them down in your engagement book. Give them priority. After a week you may not notice much difference when you use the measuring tape, even though, with a diet, you may have dropped five or six pounds. But after a month you'll be enchanted with the results. Won't it be nice to buy a lovely dress two sizes smaller and not to be ashamed to go out without a coat to hide the bulges?

For less serious problems, ten minutes morning and night will get you into trim and keep you there. Or twenty minutes once a day, if that fits your schedule better. And don't forget the while-you're-doing-something-else routines. You can be pampering your body most of the day if you remember them, and your body will be very grateful. Not to mention your husband. You can look forward to the day when the waiter says, "And what would your daughter like, sir?"

One rule: Never let your husband see you exercising. No woman rolling around on the floor looks really adorable after she's passed her third birthday.

## ORGANIZE A BEAUTY CLUB

This suggestion is for women who are short on self-discipline. In brief, lazy. I know women who pay a masseuse fifteen dollars to come in in the morning and massage them while they're still half asleep. It's much easier than getting down on the slant board or on the floor. I love massage. It won't replace sex, but its a luxurious feeling. You don't have to spend fifteen dollars a day, though, to keep a lovely body. And massage doesn't tighten up all the muscles.

Regular exercise, all alone, can be boring. If you just can't schedule it for yourself, organize a little neighborhood club. Get all those pleasingly-plump pals together *regularly* at a certain hour on certain days of the week—and compete. Competition is often just the stimulus you need.

At the first session, weigh in, take all the crucial measurements, and put them on charts. Do the weighing in and measuring every week on the same day. A woman will give up anything—from a fudge sundae to a dry martini or a grilled-cheese sandwich—to beat her fellow club members to a slim finish. She may lose a friend or two, but she'll gain loveliness, and her husband's pride and admiration. *That's* worth a couple of fat friends!

But the best thing about the club is getting down on the floor with half a dozen other women (preferably in a room with a big mirror) and seeing if you can improve faster than anyone else. There's probably nothing funnier than the sight of a row of fat women trying to touch their toes. But it's not funny for the women. It's very sad. Being fit, being the right weight, having the right proportions, can really make life a lot more fun. It's worth any device you need to achieve it.

## DIETS

There's a well-known Hollywood personality who claims that she loses weight by being hypnotized into hating the food that's bad for her. I did that to myself while I was still in my teens and saved some very big hypnotist's fees. That lady, incidentally, is still "pleasingly plump"! Maybe she doesn't keep her appointments.

Members of a club can trade diets to see which ones work. Not every diet suits all women—I suppose because of different metabolisms. I don't know. I heard of a woman who ate nothing—literally nothing—but fish. All she wanted of it. That included shellfish with a squeeze of lemon and freshly ground pepper. She lost pounds and inches faster than she could make new holes in her belts. She not only became downright skinny, she claimed that she'd never had more energy in her life. She was in her late forties. Another woman with just the same amount of overweight didn't lose an ounce on that diet.

Some people are devoted to the cottage-cheese method. Each of the three meals starts with a cup of cottage cheese. For breakfast you add a cup of fresh or canned fruit. (If it's canned, the sugary syrup should be rinsed off.) For lunch the cottage cheese is surrounded by raw vegetables—carrots, radishes, chopped cabbage, young string beans, zucchini, or asparagus. For dinner, another cup of cottage cheese with a quarter of a pound of very lean grilled meat or boiled fish or a boiled egg. You can have raw vegetable nibbles all day, and as many cups of bouillon as you like. And pickles any time. Plus a glass of buttermilk at bedtime.

This may not be as monotonous as it sounds if the dieter has an imaginative knowledge of spices and herbs to sprinkle on. I like red-pepper things, and if I tried this I know my meals would be very spicy. An all-fish diet sounds a bit dangerous to me because there are no fruits or vegetables. The thing is to be sensible and to take advantage of all the good, low-calorie things to liven up your diet menu.

Of course no diets as rigid as those should be continued for more than two weeks. Some diet "experts"—the ones who are still trying new ones because they haven't succeeded—tell you to diet five days a week and take the weekends off. I guess that's all right if you don't go berserk with chocolate éclairs and beer on Saturday and Sunday.

The really faddish diets—like subsisting solely on bananas—seem to have gone out of vogue. But there are still the all-meat diets, the all-fruit-juice diets, and even the all-carbohydrate diets. I think that any of these is an invitation to flagrant malnutrition. We need a little of everything, including some fat. The only thing it's all right to skip is starchy food, because there's a healthy amount of carbohydrate in fruits and vegetables.

Here are a few items no dieter should ever have in the house:

Peas, lima beans, avocados, olives, dried beans, corn, butter, most cheese, fatty meats, sugar, chocolate, potatoes, rice, bread, pasta, and creamed soups. The list could go on for another page or two, but any intelligent woman knows the dangerous foods.

I've never been able to understand how anyone could stand measuring out half a cup of this and four ounces of that. If a woman has the time to do that she's not busy enough—and that may be why she's overweight! It's a lot easier just to buy the foods that are fairly low in calories and to cultivate a taste for them. And have a little of each kind of essential food during the course of a day. The operative word in that bit of advice is "little." Raw nibbles, bouillon, and dill pickles always stop the hunger pangs until the next small meal is served.

## THE JOAN CRAWFORD NON-DIET

I'm often asked if I diet (I wish interviewers would come up with more original questions!). I say, "No. I just stop eating when it tastes the best."

## A Program for a Lovely Figure

I eat most of the things I like, but I eat sparingly, and I eat slowly. I simply cannot gulp down a meal. Have you ever noticed that people who eat quickly have no real interest in food, and invariably have pot bellies? I'd much rather eat the first course and forget the rest of it if it's a business lunch and everybody has to be back in forty-five minutes. Because I work under such pressure, with so many minutes here, so many minutes there, I need peace for my little meals.

When I'm filming, I get up at 5 A.M. and have a piece of fruit and a cup of tea. At 6:30, I eat an egg and bacon or sausage. I have a kitchen in my dressing room and share breakfast with my makeup man, Monty Westmore, and my hairdresser, Vivian Walker.

I eat a light lunch. Sometimes a small minute steak with two small cherry tomatoes. Sometimes chicken—boiled, not broiled. I've always found roasted or barbecued chicken incredibly dry. My chicken is boiled with carrots, celery, onions, kosher salt and pepper, and bay leaf, and it's always moist and delicious.

Sometimes I'll have some more bacon late in the afternoon. Making pictures uses up a lot of energy. In *What Ever Happened to Baby Jane?* I was supposed to be munching on a box of chocolates. Instead, I made up tiny meat balls and ate them. I eat for energy, and that means plenty of protein.

I never touch sweets. I'd much rather have a dill pickle—if I ever ate ice cream I'm sure I'd surround it with pickles. I did eat ice cream once. When I was a kid I used to run out at the first fresh snow and get cups, let it snow into the cups, then bring them in and eat the snow with sugar and cream on it. That was *my* ice cream! But now, no. I have no yearning for sweets.

I never touch potatoes because I learned a long time ago not to like what made me fat. I honestly believe that I don't like potatoes—except the little julienne shoestrings served by the Café

*203*

Chauveron. They're wisps of things cooked so all the fat and starch has been exploded out of them. I enjoy a handful of these, liberally sprinkled with salt.

If I'm lunching with tolerant friends I eat green onions, and I like to nibble on raw carrot sticks. I certainly prefer them to fancy hors d'oeuvres. Fish is a wonderful beauty food. My actress daughter Christina swears by it. I like it best straight out of the sea, when I'm in the Islands, but even frozen fish can be prepared deliciously. Many people think that cooking fish is messy, but it can be simple, and very quick.

One of my favorite methods is to layer fillets of sole with fresh salmon, pour cream of mushroom soup over it, and stick it in the oven. Use a disposable foil pan, and there's nothing messy about it at all. I like to sprinkle it with capers before serving, and surround it with lemon wedges and parsley.

I like tomatoes with a sour lemon or vinegar dressing and a sprinkling of black pepper. They give me vitamins. I keep hard-boiled eggs in the icebox all the time, and if I get terribly hungry I eat the yolk of one of them. At home I have fruit, tea, and one egg every morning. But if I've gained half a pound I give up that egg and have half an apple instead.

No, I don't diet. I eat all the things I like. In small quantities.

# ·XI·

# A Program for a Glowing Face and Lovely Hair

A LOT OF PEOPLE, even today, think you have to be rich to be beautiful. Well, if burning money is one of your hobbies there are a number of ways of doing it. Face peeling, abrasion, and face lifting head the list. Even breasts can be lifted, and fat removed from protruding stomachs—which leaves a nasty scar.

A bonanza for the undisciplined and very rich woman is the beauty farm. There, for a minor fortune, you can be starved, pummeled, and made to do setting-up exercises at sunrise. All in a lovely setting, too. Your lettuce leaf will be served on the finest porcelain.

Still more costly are sojourns with the doctors who inject live cells from animal embryos. These treatments are supposed to keep people alive (and beautiful) to extraordinary ages. The cost: about $2,000 a week plus tips. Men are among their devoted clients. Vanity isn't a matter of sex. You can spend a hundred dollars (plus tips) for a "beauty day" at a good salon, and much more if you visit a dermatologist twice a week, go to the beauty shop twice weekly (or daily for comb-outs), and call in the masseuse. A well-known skin specialist patronized by many famous beauties charges seventy-five dollars for a twenty-minute consultation and eight dollars for a cake of sea-mud soap. I get more satisfaction and just as much benefit out of applying a purée of apples and sour cream!

Your money will burn up nicely, and it isn't even the lazy way to beauty. All those visits take time, precious time. I'd hate to have to keep a two-hour beauty appointment every day or even twice a week. I wouldn't have time for other things. And I can accomplish most of what these experts do right in my own bathroom or kitchen. So can any woman. The best beauty preparations cost only a few cents and I frequently find them in my refrigerator. If they sound too simple to be effective, just try them. And then use them regularly.

## START WITH A *CLEAN* SKIN

My skin is so dry that I never use soap on it except to remove screen makeup. Then it has to have a vigorous treatment. I remove the makeup with petrolatum oil—two coats of it. Afterward I scrub with soap and water and a good heavy washcloth. And I really *scrub*. A simple pure soap does just as good a job as the perfumed, exotically packaged, high-priced ones—though I must admit I'm intrigued by the idea of soaps made with turtle oil or brown sugar.

For removing ordinary street makeup I use a good cleansing cream, and I have a set of brushes—soft, medium, and heavy— that I plug into an electric outlet so that they vibrate. They work the cream into the pores and generally stimulate the skin, bringing the blood to the surface—the skin's best nourishment. If your brushes don't plug in it doesn't matter. Just use elbow grease (good exercise for the arms) and you'll get the same results. I make sure that I get at all the makeup embedded in the hairline, around the ears, and down to wherever my dress began—because makeup should be applied over all the exposed areas, including the back of the neck, if it shows. Then I quickly apply a moisture cream.

## WATER YOUR SKIN LIKE A FLOWER

Moisturizer is probably the most blessed invention of the past two decades. Our grandmothers' skins shriveled in their forties as a result of exposure to sun and wind and harsh cosmetics. We've learned the value of watering our skins the way we water our plants, and take it for granted that we'll have a smooth glow well into our fifties, sixties, seventies—there's really no limit.

If only we would all make a habit of using moisturizer regularly. Not at bedtime. Then it only gets smeared over the pillowcases and your husband's pajamas instead of staying on your face where it will do some good. But make a habit of using it while you're working around the house, if you're a housewife. I put it on while I'm working at my desk at home. I've learned to do it especially in the wintertime because the steam heat is so terribly drying. I apply a light moisturizer before my makeup.

Treat your neck the same way you do your face. It's a delicate area, and the first to betray age. Give it the same careful cleaning, creaming, moisturizing, and stimulation.

Eye cream is very important, too. Find a brand that you like and smooth it on gently with your fingertips. Or simply use your moisturizer or some petrolatum. There's no natural oil around the eyes and those areas need to be fed to keep away tiny lines. Deep lines can't be easily erased—so don't let them develop.

Of course I use many commercial products, but I'm not devoted exclusively to any particular brand. I like one manufacturer's lipsticks for the wide range of colors, another manufacturer's moisturizer, and a third maker's mascara. My real devotion is to old-fashioned formulas and to natural foods and oils. They're still as effective as they were in Cleopatra's time.

*Looking the Part*

After showering I like one of the oldest concoctions in the world—rosewater and glycerine. I once asked a lovely lady in her eighties how she kept the skin of a baby, and that was what she used. I carry around little tubes of rosewater and glycerine to use on my hands every time I wash them, and I always work it up my arms and into my elbows. Women hardly ever look at their own elbows, but other people do! I pay attention to my knees and ankles, too. All the joints seem to dry out faster than the fleshy parts of the body.

## MASQUES

There's no better beauty treatment than a good masque, and the ones I'm going to suggest cost mere pennies. Always start with a clean, clean skin. If you have the time, stretch out on a slant board while the masque does its job, or on the floor with your feet up on a chair—thinking lovely thoughts. You might even get your telephoning done then. A masque really works only when you're lying down. Twenty minutes is the right length of time. Then wash the masque off gently with warm water and follow with a brisk splash of cold water to close the pores. A beautiful way to prepare for a beautiful evening!

Here are a few "kitchen masques" that *work:*

Mayonnaise—recommended by Rose Reti, my hair expert and authority on most things pertaining to beauty. Since I'm never sure what they put into those jars at the supermarket, I make my own with whole eggs, olive or peanut oil, and lemon juice. (Omit the salt and pepper!) Stir this until it's well blended, or whip up a batch in an electric blender.

Puréed vegetables—cucumbers, lemons, or lettuce thickened with a little baby powder.

208

Puréed fruits—cantaloupe, bananas, or strawberries mixed to a paste with milk or sour cream or honey.

Some friends of mine recommend a cod-liver oil masque for the face and neck. (Of course, all masques should cover the neck too.) And some recommend finely crushed almonds. A famous old-fashioned mixture is oatmeal, warm water, and a little honey blended to a paste.

Another mixture worth trying is unflavored gelatin beaten with witch hazel, baking soda, and a whole egg. There are debates about the relative merits of egg whites and egg yolks, but as Rose Reti says, "They're both protein. Why not use the whole egg?"

Masques should only be used once or twice a week. For a luxurious once-a-week treatment give your face a herbal steaming first by putting parsley, dill, or any other favorite herb into a pan of boiling water. (Mint is refreshing, too.) Hold a towel over your head to keep the steam rising onto your face. The pores will open so that the masque can do a better job. While the masque is working, place pads soaked in witch hazel or boric acid over your eyelids and put on your favorite music.

I haven't tried all these masques yet, but I plan to because I believe in the idea. All the ingredients I've mentioned have vitamins and minerals, or protein, and if they're good for our insides why shouldn't they nourish our skins just as well as ten-dollar formulas?

Each of these combinations has a different effect. Each one feels different. Some are soothing, some astringent. Some harden and have to be peeled off—which is good for tightening the pores. Some remain soft and lubricate the skin.

Find the combinations that feel and work best for your skin. Experiment and create your own specialty, and have the satisfaction of knowing that you are nourishing your skin from your own refrigerator and not with an unknown chemical. Europeans have known about these simple treatments for years.

Their husbands don't know about them, though, because beauty treatments should be reserved for the end of the day, *before* your husband comes home. You look awful while a masque is drying—just as awful as you do in hair curlers. And it's a myth that anything left on overnight does more good. Ten to twenty minutes is all that any good cream or preparation needs to do its job.

## HAVE A "YES" FACE

All the beauty products in the world can't disguise a disagreeable expression. Have you ever noticed that when you say "no" you begin to resemble a prune-faced schoolmarm? Not that any woman can go through life saying yes to everything, but it's a nice example of how important an expression is in giving an impression of youth.

There are more than thirty facial muscles we use for different expressions, and it's a good idea to pamper the important ones. Facial muscles can sag quickly, but there are some easy ways of keeping them toned up. Each one of the following takes just about ten seconds. You've got *that* much time!

1. Open your mouth as wide as you can and at the same time purse your lips as if you're trying to whistle. Hold it for ten seconds.

2. Put your thumb and forefinger inside your mouth and try to push your fingers out—at the same time forcing your cheeks *in*. Hold for another count of ten.

For heaven's sake be sure you're alone when you do these, because you'll look ridiculous. But they do keep important facial muscles in good condition. I know a lady executive who does them in the taxi every morning on her way to her office. I'd love to hear what some of those taxi drivers are thinking!

## MAKEUP

Men hate too much makeup. They're afraid it will rub off on them. And you know something? It does.

After a certain age makeup should be called "make down." Too much of it is aging. I use the same makeup for day and evening, and always do the job in strong daylight. If it's a rainy day I use cold or white lights—never yellow, because it turns your blues a different color. I have a large mirror facing a window, and white lights on the top and sides. This gives me a much more subtle makeup, so that when I go out in sunlight I look all right. And if I happen to be taken to a dark restaurant no one can see what color lipstick I have on anyway.

The thing I can't stand—and so many women are guilty of it— is to see makeup that stops at the chinline. Maybe it's because they're afraid it will spoil their turtlenecks, but it's awful to see that line of demarcation at the jaw. I always take a profile look to see if there's a stop line on the neck. The neck is part of the face when it comes to cosmetics, and they should be tapered down to wherever the dress starts.

A lovely girl I know in Hollywood has beautiful skin, but she used to appear with the worst makeup job I've ever seen. She put very dark suntan powder over her beautiful white skin and it stopped right at the chin. It was too damned heavy, and the wrong color. And she had a white neck. I sent her to the studio makeup man and paid for two sessions so that she could learn what to do with that lovely face. Now she's using a more subtle base, blending it well, and covering it with translucent powder, used sparingly. I use a powder with an ivory bisque base that suits my skin tone. After powdering, take a tissue and *blot*. Then clothes won't be soiled.

Achieving that casual "under-made-up" effect takes more time than it did in the garish forties when we used such bright colors. The shades you use depend on your complexion and to some extent on where you are. There are makeup kits with graduated shades of base, lipstick, eyeshadow, and so forth, so that when you go into a warm climate and get a touch of the sun you can adjust to your skin tones. They are useful in the transition months, too—spring to summer, summer to fall. I often use them when I'm on a tour for Pepsi that takes me from one hemisphere to another.

### CREATE A NEW FACE

If God gave you some uneven features you can redesign your face to some extent. I used to depend on Monty Westmore, my makeup man at the studio, for that kind of artistry, but any woman can reshape her face, create an illusion. She can bring up the cheekbones, soften a too-square chin, slim a too-wide nose— in short, ring all sorts of structural changes.

The rule is: Lighter shades emphasize features; darker shades minimize them.

Start with your base. Bases come in convenient stick form, but I prefer a liquid one. A sallow skin needs a pinkish tone. For a ruddy complexion, beige is flattering. Smooth the base right up to the hairline (you can always wipe spots off the hair with a tissue later) and blend it around the ears, on the earlobe, and down over the neck.

If your face is very round, smooth a darker shade at the sides, below the cheekbone, to narrow it. If your nose is too long, put the darker shade at the tip, and at the sides of the nostrils. There are a number of possibilities, depending on your bone structure.

A lighter shade will bring out receding features. If you haven't as much chin as you'd like, smooth a pale base over it. Use pale pink just under the brow and under the eyes to bring out deep-set eyes. I don't use white under my brows because my bone structure doesn't lend itself to that. But many women look better with this eye highlighter. I hate to see girls with *too* much white under the brow—or too much eye makeup of any kind, for that matter. If the forehead protrudes they shouldn't use the white under the brows at all. It exaggerates it. And if they have a tendency to be puffy—and everybody has puffy days—they look worse with great white blobs under the eyes.

The important thing about shading and contouring is to blend so carefully that you can never see where one shade ends and the other begins. If you have a problem at first, go to the best beauty shop in your vicinity and have a lesson or two. I've sent several girls to experts to be taught how to make up. You can learn at home, though, in front of a daylight mirror. By trial and error you'll see how to bring out your best features and minimize the worst.

So start with three shades of base for the redesigning, plus white if you need it. Add a blusher that you brush on with a large soft brush made for the purpose. I like a light brownish shade. It matches my natural complexion and I brush it on under my cheekbones to accent my bone structure. But a very fair skin could use a bluish pink blusher and, at the other extreme, an olive skin should have a warm brown one.

Translucent powder goes on next. It must be translucent or your careful job of shading will be covered over. And not too much. Just a light dusting of it to cover the shine, and then blot the excess.

Then lipstick. I try new shades all the time. My dressing table contains a wide range of colors because I have such a range of dresses in pinks, Chinese red, oranges and dozens of shades in between that the precise color of my lipstick is very important. For beige costumes, of course, it matters less. I put on the lipstick and smooth it over with my finger—I never rub my lips together. Then I outline the lips carefully with a lipstick pencil. I never use a brush. Then *blot*. There's nothing uglier than lipstick on the teeth.

## EYE MAKEUP

Makeup should be just a frame for the eyes. When you lay on all the bright-colored goop and slather white under the brows the eyes themselves are lost in camouflage. Just accent whatever God has given you with a subtle hand. The more makeup a woman applies after forty the older she looks. And yet so many overdo it just because young girls can. They wear that bright turquoise shadow and look as if they're going to a Halloween party.

I never wear shadow of any kind. I use a liner, mascara, and very delicate false lashes. For daytime I cut out every other lash to lighten the effect. For evening I use them as they come.

The liner goes on first, and then I brush my own upper lashes with mascara. Putting on the false lashes takes a little practice. I take the lash near the base with a pair of tweezers, apply the liquid adhesive, and center it at the very edge of my eyelid. Then I use the tweezers to ease down the outer edge, and then the inner one, working toward the nose. A little more mascara on both my own and the false lashes blends them together and makes them look natural.

Finally, I brush my brows. They're naturally heavy and dark and only need brushing to keep them neat and to remove any powder that might have got caught in them.

Early in my career I had plucked and plucked so that I'd have those spindly little lines that were the fashion then. When eyebrows came back a lot of girls found that they couldn't grow them any more. They'd plucked out the roots.

I encouraged new growth by using castor oil and yellow vaseline—half and half—and rubbing it the wrong way, toward the nose, with a brush. I still use it, and it makes the brows grow

215

*When makeup became more feminine and sensuous, we let our eye-
brows grow and let our lips be full and natural.*

like mad. It's good for lashes, too, but I always get the oil in my
eyes, then they water and turn red. Brows frame the eyes. Encourage them, for they're a great beauty asset.

This reads like a long, painstaking process, but after practice a complete makeup job can be done in just a few minutes. With the quick changes I have to make, I *know* how fast it can be done! The end product should be a very natural look. A soft, romantic one that a man wants to reach out and touch. I think we're finished with that "Hey! Look at me!" makeup. We want to be feminine and very touchable, and have people say, "You've come a long way, baby!"

## HAIR—ITS LOVING CARE

I have my hair colored. I was born a redhead—all my freckles are proof of that. I have it tinted now to a muted reddish blond. It suits my skin tones, and it makes me feel happy. Rose Reti, who now has her own shop, first did my coloring thirty years ago, when I was living in New York. She came once or twice to Hollywood, but it was after I moved back to New York about sixteen years ago that she began doing it all the time. We've gone through quite a few shades together.

Once I let the coloring grow out. I cut my hair short as a boy's and went down to Jamaica where, with the sun and the salt water, it grew very rapidly. Then I found white and dark streaks. I wore it that way, salt and pepper, for about a year, but I found I was throwing away all my beige clothes—giving them away—because they were designed for a redhead. I began buying everything gray. So I started to think gray! I said to myself, "This is ridiculous. I refuse to think gray!" So I had it bleached to the shade I wear now.

That salt-and-pepper was great for a couple of pictures. It gave my face a great deal of character and strength. But it did something to me mentally, to my spirits, that I just didn't like.

Lightening the hair softens the face, and a mature woman needs that. You can't go against nature, but you can improve on it. Very dark hair is harsh. My original carrot-top shade wouldn't do for me now. It has to be toned down. Naturally dark hair should be taken down to a soft brown. Tallulah Bankhead's sister did that and Rose Reti said it gave her a very soft look.

## Coloring

Hair should be a little darker in front, around the face, but it should never be more than four or five shades from the natural color. All the tones should be blended. An exception to the rule is in TV or filming, where very light hair around the face makes an actress look as if she's halfway bald. I know a young actress who has very dark hair and a snow-white streak that makes her look as if she's wearing a headband on screen. I like a subtle blend from one shade to another to give highlights but preserve a soft, natural look.

A woman should pick the right shade very carefully. It's worth paying to get expert advice about this. You can also get a good idea of what shades are becoming by trying on wigs. See which do the most for your complexion. A ruddy skin tone looks best with cool shades without a hint of red. A sallow skin is flattered with a light hair color. Olive skin needs hair color with gold highlights.

If you plan to do your own coloring, experiment first with temporary rinses before you risk a permanent job that will take time to grow out. After you've found the right coloring process, be scrupulous about keeping up with the roots. Most women need a touchup once a month. I have to have mine done every ten days, *at least*. My hair grows very quickly, and if I go into a hot climate the sun brings out a darker red than I like to have. Watch it. There's nothing uglier than roots that don't match the rest of your hair.

*I like to be able to vary my hairstyle with my mood.*

Hair that has been colored is susceptible to the sun. It's best to keep it covered with a scarf or a pretty hat. Sun isn't kind to the skin, either, even though a tan is so attractive. After a woman reaches thirty she should get her tan out of a bottle—with a good base—and protect her skin and hair from the direct rays of the summer sun.

## Looking the Part

A woman with coarse hair and dark eyes can go all white to get a "big" look. But with fine hair or light-colored eyes white hair is simply aging. It needs a very fair complexion, too.

Coloring doesn't damage hair. In fact, the best color products have built-in conditioners that are helpful. It's medication that does the damage. Pills. Diet pills, tranquilizers, pep pills—all the drugs that most of us should manage to live without. They produce sick hair.

## Teasing and Spraying

Teasing and back-combing is bad. I'm glad that most women have stopped doing it. It splits and breaks the hair and then the color can't go in properly and it can't be groomed well. If hair needs building up, a fall is the best way to do it, combing your own hair over the front and sides to get height and a natural look at the same time.

Hair spray is sheer poison. At a medical convention some time ago doctors said that if women continue to tease their hair and spray it to the degree that they've been doing, within ten years they will be totally bald! I believe this. Also, a man going to bed with a woman with a tremendous bouffant hairdo must suffocate. The smell is overpowering. A very funny story was going around a few years ago. The definition of a nymphomaniac: any woman who goes to bed with her husband after having spent the day in a beauty salon.

Besides being unromantic, hair spray is the cause of respiratory problems. When I came down with pneumonia while I was doing a film, the first thing the doctors asked was, "Do you use hair spray?"

They feel that spray is harmful in the way that tobacco smoke is—or any kind of pollution. It makes a plastic coating on the throat. When I have to be sprayed for television I go out into the hallway, cover my face, and hold my breath while they're doing it. Then I go back to my dressing room where that poison isn't floating around. The skin inhales it. And I only use it when I'm on television.

I wish that hair spray wasn't so lethal, because my hair is baby fine. Rose has given me a wonderful conditioner that gives it body, but it's still a problem. A good cut helps fine hair. With an expert cut it will fall into the right place most of the time. Fresh beer helps in setting it. It does not leave an odor or a residue, and it does help give some body. But conditioning is the most important thing. Hair should be luxuriant, shiny, and spanking clean. It should make a man want to run his fingers through it.

### Nourish Your Hair

There are a number of "kitchen recipes" for feeding the hair. It needs the contents of your refrigerator just as much as your skin does. Right back to mayonnaise! Olive oil, eggs, and lemon juice. Massage the mixture into your hair, let it stay on for ten or fifteen minutes, then rinse it off with cool water. Cool—or you'll have scrambled eggs on your head.

For years I washed my daughters' hair with raw eggs, never soap or shampoo. I wet their hair first and then rubbed in six whole eggs, one by one—a trick I learned from Katharine Hepburn. (Four eggs will do for short hair, but theirs was long.) Some people use eggs beaten up with a jigger of rum; others mix an egg with red wine. Hot oil is good for dry hair. Apply it with the fingertips and then wrap your head in a warm towel. Keep changing the oil for an hour, to keep it hot and penetrating. Then shampoo. Cologne massaged into the scalp is a help for oily hair

—a problem I don't have. And tea and vinegar are recommended for bringing out natural highlights.

I believe in brushing. I made my girls give their hair the old-fashioned hundred strokes every night, using two brushes, and bending forward from the waist. It stimulates hair growth, and the rush of blood to the face is an added benefit. I pull my hair gently to encourage growth, too.

## Styling

As for styling—no book can tell you what style is best for the shape of your face, the texture of your hair, or your way of life. For some women it's a smooth, beautifully groomed chignon caught low on the neck. (The length of the neck should be taken into consideration, too.) For others an upswept hairdo is both chic and flattering—and it shows off lovely earrings. For still others a good short cut with flattering little wisps or fringes is most attractive. I don't think any woman over thirty-five should wear a long pageboy, or very straight hair, at all—her hair should be a little softer.

Look back at those candid snapshots again. Does your hair look like the elegant woman of the seventies? If not, look through some of the hair-styling and fashion magazines. Pick one or two styles you think would be appropriate and try them. Keep trying until you find the right one. And don't forget to look at both profiles and the back of your head in the mirror before you go out. Everyone else will see them.

*I always make up in daylight when I can; otherwise, with white fluorescent light.*

## A TOUCH OF MAGIC

Millions of words can be written—and have been—about how to look lovely. But there's a final element that no amount of exercising, dieting, or mirror watching can give you. Charm.

Charm isn't something you can turn on like a tap with a pretty little-girl simper. It isn't anything phony that you can pick up at the door on your way out, along with your coat. You know, animals can spot a phony faster than most people. I mistrust people who don't like animals or understand them: how one dog can be snooty, one cat imperious, one dog beguiling, one cat sitting there quietly checking on you. Any wise little cat or dog knows at a glance whether your charm is real or manufactured for the occasion—and treats you accordingly.

Charm is an ease with people—all kinds of people. I've never known anyone blessed with it like Maurice Chevalier, for instance, who always has been completely at ease and consequently puts *you* at ease. And Ronald Colman had the greatest charm I've ever known. Even if there were a hundred people in the room he never spoke above a very low tone.

Remember that lovely line from "Desiderata": "Avoid loud and aggressive persons; they are vexatious to the spirit . . ."

But charm is not only being soft-spoken, relaxed, and at ease; it's wanting to be a giver. Wanting to be a good listener. Responding, communicating, having a genuine interest in people. It's having a good memory for amusing things so that you're a happy person to be with.

Charm is grace—graciousness. And it all has to be real—good manners *and* good manners of the heart.

Charm is a touch of magic. Try to make it a part of *your* way of life.

224